RAINY DAYS AND STARRY NIGHTS

GROWING UP IN THE
SOUTH TEXAS BRUSH COUNTRY

Margaret, Lawrence Jr. and Lois Zook at home in 1950.

Rainy Days and Starry Nights

Growing Up in the
South Texas Brush Country

Lois Zook Wauson

MAVERICK PUBLISHING COMPANY

MAVERICK PUBLISHING COMPANY
P.O. Box 6355, San Antonio, Texas 78209

Library of Congress Cataloging-in-Publication Data

Wauson, Lois Zook, 1932-
   Rainy days and starry nights : growing up in the South Texas Brush Country / Lois Zook Wauson.
      p. cm.
   ISBN 1-893271-30-7
   1. Wauson, Lois Zook, 1932– 2. Farm life–Texas–Wilson County. 3. Wilson County (Tex.)–Biography. 4. San Antonio (Tex.)–Biography. I. Title.
   CT275.W335A3 2003
   976.4'445–dc22

                                        2003017739

Printed in theUnited States of America on acid-free paper

5 4 3 2 1

Cover: Gathered on a Brush Country road in 1942.
Back cover: Margaret, Lois and Elizabeth Zook at the old farmhouse.

Contents

Preface

Dense brush and low mesquite trees flourish in untended stretches of the sandy South Texas plains of Wilson County. Its biggest town is Floresville, the county seat, 30 miles southeast of San Antonio. Floresville, with 5,000 people now, is also known as the Peanut Capital of Texas.

I grew up in southwestern Wilson County, where our post office address was McCoy. My childhood happened to coincide with the difficult days of the Depression of the 1930s and early 40s, and, in the first half of the 1950s, of the worst drought in the recorded history of Texas. They were not easy years for a large family trying to survive on a small farm.

But my parents, Lawrence and Bertie Lee Zook, instilled in us the importance not of money or material things but of love, commitment and hard work. Because of that love, long after our parents are gone we are still very close. My husband and I moved from San Antonio to North Texas in 1968, but I still cherish the memory of those early years.

I'd like to dedicate this book to my parents and to my seven brothers and sisters, Margaret, Lawrence Jr., Elizabeth, Bob, Gerry, Don and Sam, whom I love very much.

I also want to thank my husband, Eddie, and our children, Trent, Julie, Derek and Kristi, for encouraging me to do this book.

I especially want to thank Kristi for giving me the opportunity to write a column of reminiscences for her weekly newspaper in the Hill Country town of Leakey. She guided me, corrected my mistakes and always gave me hope that I could write better. I would like to thank the Floresville *Chronicle-Journal* for also carrying my column, from which this book has evolved.

1. Rainy Days Were the Best Days

Daddy was rugged and big, and used cuss words. He rolled his own cigarettes. He always seemed to be wearing a straw hat, and to smell of sweat and dirt. He didn't shave very often. When he would nuzzle my cheek to give me a kiss, if he was in a good mood, his whiskers scratched like everything.

He was gruff, tough and hard, and his hands were huge. I knew what those big hands felt like and also the belt he would take off and use on us. It didn't take much to set off that anger and violence.

He was angry, worried and engrossed with farming and with making a living on our 100 acres of sandy farmland and pastures with scrubby mesquite trees and lots of cactus. I was scared of him. When I heard his loud, angry voice yelling at my mother or my brothers and sisters and me I trembled with fear and tried to get out of the way. He always seemed to be in a bad mood.

It's funny how weather has such an effect on our lives, especially for farmers and ranchers. Their life depends on whether it rains or doesn't rain, or if the weather is too hot or too cold. Daddy's moods depended on the weather.

His family says he inherited that temper from his father, Samuel Zook, a preacher who spoke Spanish, established Methodist missions in the Rio Grande Valley and came to Floresville to start its Spanish Methodist Church. He ruled his family with an iron hand. My grandmother, a gentle woman, helped balance out family relationships.

My mother was the same way, though she could use a peach tree switch on us with vigor and strength. We didn't get away with much.

Daddy and Mother as they began married life on the farm.

Daddy loved farming. He came from a long line of farmers in Kansas, and in Pennsylvania way before that. After graduating from Floresville High School in 1919 he went to Kansas State for a year and played football, then went to work in an uncle's orange groves in California.

He came back to the Zook farm in Wilson County in 1924, when his mother was dying, and took over after his father died four years later. He sold the old farm in 1936 and bought our farm a few miles away.

He tried to make a living there for 20 more years. Most of those years he struggled with drought, low farm prices and the Depression, boll weevils, grasshoppers and other things that plague farmers. He raised cotton, corn, maize, peanuts, watermelons and, one year, black-eyed peas.

I wish Daddy could have had one good year of farming. I wish there could have been one year when it was raining at the right time, the sun was shining at the right time and the banker was being paid on time. But there wasn't, and in 1957 he finally gave up and left the farm.

He and my mother moved to a small duplex near Stinson Field in San Antonio, taking my baby brother Sammy, the only child still at home. They moved a few more times over the next 30 years, finally settling on Heather Street, but the house on Irwin Drive had the best garden and flowers.

The next 30 years were much better than the first, but Daddy never lost his love for the land. He still had lush gardens and flowers. He had a green thumb. But he also had water from a faucet. During those years he began to mellow. He lost most of the anger that was there in those early years.

As I've grown older, I've begun to understand his frustration, and the worry and fear of losing everything. During those years of farming he would see his crops literally burn up in the fields. He didn't have enough money to make the yearly mortgage payment, so he'd have to take out another loan for seed and start new crops.

Year after year this happened. I am sure he worried about how he was going to feed his large family. During the Depression he left for weeks to work for WPA, leaving Mother to cope with the farm and the kids.

I can still see him standing on the edge of the cornfield watching rain clouds gather. If they passed by he would turn, walk toward the house and yell at us kids to come start the milking, feeding, gathering eggs and all the chores. He would be talking to himself, cussing under his breath, his face angry and hard. We scurried to get to work, not wanting to face that anger. We knew any little thing would set him off. Better to not say a word.

But the times it rained! Daddy would yell at Mother, "Bertie Lee, how about parching some peanuts out yonder?" ("Dad-gum" and "out yonder" were his favorite words to throw into a story he was telling, or throw into any conversation he was having, for that matter.) From a burlap sack in the closet Mother would pour a large roasting pan full of Spanish peanuts and put them in the oven to roast.

After they were ready, Daddy would sit on the porch in the big old wooden rocking chair with a pan full of peanuts, cracking them open and popping them into his mouth and laughing and singing songs for us. We'd sit on the steps eating peanuts, too, looking up at him, so happy because Daddy was in a good mood. It

Mother and Daddy in 1965, eight years after they left the farm.

was raining! He would smile and call us "scalawags" or "snicklefritz." He would call Mother "sweetheart" or "darlin' " during those times.

Most of the time, though, he was mad and called her "woman." When he said, "Woman, what did you do with all the money?" after coming home from buying groceries in town, or "Woman, where are my work pants?" I knew it was time to run for the barn and hide.

But when it was raining, he was happy and laughing. Oh, if it could rain all the time!

After the hard ground around our house softened with rain and was smooth and slick, we girls ran out with sticks and began to draw in the dirt. We became great artists. Then we sat, piling the wet sand on our feet and building sand castles, houses, garages for our cars. We made roads and highways of flat, empty vanilla and liniment and medicine bottles. The air smelled like fresh rain, and we loved it.

In his later years when he and Mother had steady jobs, money wasn't so much of a problem. His life was easier. He loved his garden and flowers, going to church, visiting with old friends, having his kids and grandkids come over to visit. He was so proud of all of them. He and Mother took trips all over Texas to visit family. They went to Kansas one year, taking a few grandchildren with them. Gone was most of the anger, frustration and worry.

And he still loved to talk. He was an avid reader of newspapers, listened to the radio and seemed to know everything about anything and to want to talk about it.

He had an advantage with Hispanics because he could speak Spanish, too. When Mr. Ximenez came by to visit we could hear Daddy talking loudly in broken Spanish and English. Somehow Mr. Ximenez understood him, but I'm not sure he ever got to say anything unless Daddy took a breath and Mr. Ximenez could jump in.

Mother and Daddy celebrated their 50th anniversary in 1981. He died in 1984, at the age of 82. My mother had stuck it out all those years, enduring the hard times, the anger and frustration, and she made it to the last half, much better than the first.

Mother said to me once, a few years before she died, in 1994, "You know, all I have left are the good memories, because God has erased all the bad memories. Now, I can remember those good times so much clearer than the bad times."

That is the way I feel now. God has left me with all these wonderful, good memories of my father. Those other memories, the bad ones, are very dim, because now I understand my father, and also know what forgiveness does for you. It has left me a heart and memories that have been healed.

I love stormy days and the sound of thunder and rain, because of all the good memories I have from when it rained on the farm.

2. Saturdays on the Farm

We sat out on the front steps as the sun began to dip over the trees in the west. The sky slowly flared with yellows and reds, reflecting off the scattered clouds. We knew what that meant: No rain.

"Red sky at night, sailor's delight! Red sky in the morning, sailor's take warning!"

Oh well, let's keep our eyes on the direction of the dirt road coming from town. Mother and Daddy surely will be coming soon.

It was Saturday on the farm. We loved Saturdays—except during harvest season, when everyone worked through the weekends—because on Saturdays Mother and Daddy went to Floresville. Sometimes all the kids went along with them. But most of the time we stayed home, cleaned the house and did our chores.

We girls spent the mornings making the house spic and span. We did dishes, made the beds, put things away, swept the linoleum floors and mopped every room till there wasn't a speck of dirt in the house. The boys, along with some of the girls, cleaned up and swept the yard, since we had a dirt lawn.

We also did those things we weren't supposed to do when they were not home, like jumping off the top of the barn into a pile of hay. The barn was at least 50 feet high. As I stood there staring down onto the top of the haystack, at least 20 feet away from the barn, my heart was in my throat. If I jumped too short, I would hit the ground and break my leg, or worse.

I quit thinking about it and jumped. It was exhilarating to fly through the air and land in the pile of hay. One

Gathered on a Brush Country road in 1942, from left, Lois, 10, holding Donny, 1; Bob, 5; Lawrence Jr., 8; Margaret, 9; Gerry, 3; and Elizabeth, 7.

by one, we kids would dare each other to jump. I think we all jumped with no injuries.

We also went down into the pasture and, taking along some matches, some links of sausage and homemade bread, gathered up dead branches and built a fire down by the creek. It's a wonder we didn't set the pasture on fire, since there was a drought most of the time.

Cooking the sausage on a stick and putting it between two pieces of bread was the highlight of the afternoon; we hoped Mother wouldn't notice the sausage missing from the smokehouse—there weren't many links left from the winter. Then we'd play cowboys and Indians. With a bunch of kids it was easy to choose sides. We had some pretty brutal wars down there in the pasture.

Coming back, we did evening chores like milking and feeding the hogs, chickens and livestock and gathering the eggs, then sat out front watching for our parents to come home. We knew they'd bring goodies like ice for the old icebox sitting in the kitchen. If the ice had run out the day before it was still cool in the box, but it needed ice quickly. Maybe they'd make ice cream when they came.

As it got dark, it was hard to see across the fields to the road, so we watched for the lights of cars. Sometimes the boys would get on the roof of the house so they could be the first to see car lights beaming over the hill. "Here they come," they would shout. We would all stand up and watch anxiously as the lights slowly came down the road and got to the mailbox at the end of our lane, but then they often disappeared and went on. We would sit back down, disappointed.

We passed the time singing songs like "You Are My Sunshine," "When the Work's All Done This Fall" or "Cowboy Jack," which Aunt Sally and Aunt Fay taught us the summers they came to visit from San Antonio.

Our bellies would begin to rumble, because we were hungry. What would Mother bring special to fix for supper? I was tired of cornbread and milk for supper, oatmeal or cornmeal mush for breakfast and vegetables from our garden for lunch. We always had milk, eggs and vegetables. We never went hungry on the farm during the Depression, like a lot of city folks did, but sometimes we yearned for something store-bought, like a loaf of light bread, bologna, salami, a box of corn flakes or fruit like oranges and apples and grapes. We had a few peaches, but fresh fruit was a delicacy.

Finally, the beam of headlights we'd watched coming across the field would turn into our lane and slowly come toward our house. We all jumped up and squealed and ran to meet them. Excitedly, we helped bring in the paper bags filled with groceries.

The fun of going through the bags was like Christmas morning. I liked best a huge bag of ginger snaps. Later on we'd help Mother make a large pitcher of lemonade with ice chipped from the 50-pound block they'd brought wrapped in a burlap sack.

When Mother looked around the house and exclaimed how nice everything looked, we were really glad we'd cleaned everything up. When we'd picked a bunch of wildflowers and put them in a jar on the dining room table, she'd go over and sniff them and smile, as she put on her apron to start supper.

I'd sit on the front steps with a fruit jar filled with iced lemonade and a handful of ginger snaps. I felt like I was in Heaven.

Mother would be in the kitchen sometimes cooking up a big pot of spaghetti for supper, and I could smell the aroma of the sauce. We didn't have spaghetti very often. I knew she'd used some jars of her own canned tomatoes and added all her own spices. She'd make the sauce and pour it in the pot with the cooked spaghetti and mix it all up. For a family of nine or ten, she had to make a big pot. My mouth watered just thinking about that first bite.

While Mother was cooking, Daddy would be out back preparing the ice cream. When our old wooden ice cream freezer was broken he used a large tin milk bucket, packed it with ice and salt and used a gallon syrup bucket in the middle full of the vanilla ice cream base Mother mixed up. All of us kids took turns turning the gallon bucket back and forth, holding onto the wire handle. It was very tiring, but, with so many of us, we kept it going.

Finally it was ready. Daddy would pack it down good with burlap bags to harden it. After supper we'd all sit out in the back yard on the steps or on the bed of the wagon eating the ice cream, spooned out in cereal bowls.

The night was perfect. The stars were so bright in the night sky, the gulf breeze kicked up from the south and sometimes there was a half moon shining in the sky. I could hear the cows lowing in the pens by the barn, a whippoorwill calling in the night, an old owl hooting down in the pasture.

I loved Saturdays.

3. The Day My Parents Eloped

It was a common practice in the Depression days for couples to just run off and get married. There was not much money for big weddings, so a couple would many times just go into town to the nearest preacher or justice of the peace, get married and go home, with no big fanfare or celebration.

My parents, Bertie Lee Goode and Lawrence Zook, eloped this way.

Bertie Lee was scared of her father. He knew she was being courted by Lawrence, but he wasn't ready for any of his children to marry. Although she was 20 years old and had a mind of her own, her father was boss in the home, and she loved and respected her father.

As Bertie Lee would tell her side of the story many years later, she thought maybe it was because she was such a hard worker. The oldest of ten children, she worked in the fields, picking cotton and helping during hay season and also helping take care of the younger ones. Her mother, Lavonia, was expecting another baby soon and relied on her a lot.

Lawrence was a handsome bachelor, 30 years old, and lived down the road. He became good friends with Mother's younger brother, William, 19. William went to dances and into town with Lawrence and came back telling of Lawrence's travels to Kansas, California and places Bertie Lee only dreamed of. And he had been to college! She thought he was so debonair and good looking.

Several months after she'd seen him from a distance chasing his pigs down at his farm she called him "that hog farmer." She didn't want anything to do with him.

Finally, on New Years Eve in 1930, Lawrence and William asked her to go with them to a dance. With his hat cocked over his eye, his overcoat on and muffler thrown around his neck, she thought Lawrence was the handsomest man she had ever seen.

The courtship went on for several months. Finally they decided to elope. Bertie Lee was afraid to tell anyone. The day before they got married, Lawrence went into Floresville along with William to buy her wedding dress. This had to be done in secret. Bertie Lee had to trust that Lawrence knew what to pick out.

He bought a beautiful silk flowered dress that hung just below her knees. It was just what she wanted. She felt like a princess. She changed at a friend's house, and that night—May 27, 1931—they went into Floresville to get married by a justice of the peace. William was the best man.

Bertie Lee spent her wedding night at Lawrence's house. Everyone in the Goode family knew what must have happened. No one said a word. She was always home early, but not one person in the Goode family talked about why she hadn't come home.

The next morning a car came up the lane. Bertie Lee's black hair was flying in the wind and her yellow flowered wedding dress fluttering. Lawrence's hat tilted on the side of his head. The newlyweds broke the news to the family. No one was surprised.

Bertie Lee's younger sisters thought she looked so pretty, and they were so jealous. Some of the older ones were miffed because Bertie Lee wasn't there to help with the chores and take care of the younger ones. Even Bertie Lee later said she felt guilty leaving her mother with all those kids and work to do.

What they didn't realize was that Bertie Lee hadn't really left work and drudgery behind but had acquired a lot more responsibility. She was marrying a farmer, and the next 25 years were the hardest years of her life. The Depression days were ahead, and the drought-stricken years of the '40s and '50s. She also had eight children.

Mother and me beside our house.

But just as she feared, her father was very angry. Several weeks after the wedding he got into a fight with Lawrence, who hit him. Earl Goode didn't speak to him for nearly a year. He wouldn't go near their farm but would go to the gate, and if Bertie Lee wanted to see him she could come down to the gate. She became pregnant right away, but the two men did not speak until the day the baby was born, nine months later.

That night Earl Goode drove over to the Zook farm, went in the house and shook Lawrence's hand, then held his first grandchild. The two men sat and looked at a tiny baby's face, taking turns holding her, forgetting all their bitterness and unforgivingness.

From that time on, the men stayed friends until Earl Goode died more than 30 years later. A baby had brought reconciliation to a family.

That baby was me.

4. The Old Black Iron Pot

The large, black iron pot that stood in our back yard for years served many purposes.

Mother and Daddy brought it in the wagon in 1936 when we moved from the Camp Ranch community to the Kasper community. We washed clothes in it for many years. We carried water to the kettle from the cistern near the house if it had rainwater in it. If not, we had to haul water in large barrels from an artesian well on a farm miles away.

A fire had to be built under the pot. We had to keep adding wood so it would not smoke too much. From the kettle she would take buckets of water and pour them into large washtubs on a bench nearby. Using rub boards to scrub and clean the clothes and the lye soap she made every winter, she scrubbed the dirty clothes and put them into another tub with rinse water. If the weather was cold, she poured a little boiling water from the black pot into the rinse water.

If the clothes were really dirty and needed soaking, they would be put into the kettle to boil for an hour or so. Then she rinsed the wash, wrung it out by hand and hung it on the clotheslines. As my sisters and I grew older we were required to help with this weekly chore.

My favorite time of year to use the black cast iron pot was during "hog killing weather." When the first really cold norther blew in we knew it was hog killing time, an exciting time on our farm.

Early in the morning a fire was started under the pot and brought to a boil. Fires were also built under large barrel drums and filled with water. As Daddy started out to the pasture where the pigpens were I could see the .22 rifle under his arm, and I knew in a few minutes I would hear a shot, the part I dreaded. I would hold my ears and run in the house.

Later, my brother Junior would call, "Lois they're coming, they have the hog. Come on out!" They drove up in a wagon with the hog lying on the floorboards.

Hogs are not skinned like cattle, but the hair must be scraped off. There were usually some neighbors to help. They would tie the carcass and, using a large block-and-tackle, hang it up by the hind legs from a tree, then slowly drop the carcass head-first into the boiling water, going up and down until the hog's hair was softened enough to begin the process of scraping. As we got a little older, all of us kids had to help.

Later, the men would remove the head and entrails and hang the carcass to drain. Afterward, they would cut it into hams, shoulders, pork chops and ribs. We had a hand-powered grinder to make sausage. The part I hated was making the sausage casings ourselves. These were made from the entrails, which were cleaned and boiled for a long time. In later years I think they did buy them at the store. I was so glad. That was a gross job.

Still, the best remembrances are the smell of the smoking fires in the smokehouse, as Mother and Daddy would hang the hams, which had been covered with brown sugar, to be smoked. I loved the sight and smell of the rows of sausages hanging from the rafters.

We helped mother stuff the sausage, which she mixed in huge pans, adding sage and other seasonings. Our job was to turn the grinder handle as another child held the casing to the spout as we put the sausage through. Then Mother or Daddy tied a string on the end and piled it in a large pan to be hung in the smokehouse. To this day I love the taste of smoked pork sausage; it still brings back how the smokehouse looked and smelled like inside.

Several days later, the old black pot was used to make lye soap. Mother put scraps of pork skins and pork fat in the kettle and rendered the fat from the skins. Next the fat was strained and returned to the kettle. Then she added lye and cooked the mixture over a slow fire, stirring it with a large wooden paddle.

When it started to thicken they would either remove the fire or allow it to die. Then the soap was dipped out and put into pans to harden so it could be cut in a usable size. The soap was used for laundry, but sometimes, if we ran out of Lifebuoy soap, we used it for bathing.

Sometimes we used the big kettle to boil water when we were killing chickens and needed to dunk them in hot water so the feathers could be plucked easily. If Mother needed a lot of chickens for canning, we used the kettle. If she needed only a few, she would boil the water in a smaller kettle in the kitchen, on her big black cast iron cooking woodstove. Our job was to pluck the chickens.

I had to help in killing them, chopping off their heads with an ax. This was not a job I wanted or liked, and I tried to get out of it when I could. I have no idea how I did that chore. Today I refuse to even cut up a chicken I buy at the market.

I think Mother left that old black kettle on the farm when they moved away. She loved modern new conveniences, like washing machines and being able to buy meat at the grocery store instead of butchering it herself at home, and she never wanted to go back to that lifestyle.

When I see large black cast iron kettles full of flowers in people's front yards, I wonder if they realize what the history of the old pot is. You know, filling it with beautiful flowers instead of boiling water for butchering hogs, dirty clothes, lye soap and chicken feathers probably makes the old iron kettles very happy, sort of like turning an old workhorse into a beautiful steed, or an ugly duckling into a swan.

5. Sister Agatha Linn

Her black nun's habit flying in the wind as she rounded the bases in a game of baseball with her nieces and nephews, Sister Agatha Linn was a sight. She would come to the Zook family reunions every Labor Day weekend at my Uncle Warren Zook's place on the San Antonio River. She always brought a companion, a young girl who was beautiful and fun to have around. They used to bring guitars and sing for us, too.

To us kids these nuns were mysterious women with a secret life totally different from ours. Though we never went to church, living so far out in the country, they were fascinating to us. I used to wonder what they wore under those long black gowns. And how about their hair—did they cut it real short?

Her name wasn't always Sister Agatha Linn. It used to be Gladys Zook. She was one of Daddy's three sisters. None had any children. One time, before she became a nun, Aunt Gladys tried to take me away from my family and adopt me.

The "kidnapping" incident was in 1937. She came driving up one August from Brownsville, near the Mexican border, to visit and stay a few days. When she left she asked if I could come visit her for a while.

As Mother told me in later years, when she would finally talk about it, she was very nervous about letting me go. I had never been away from home. I was five, Margaret was four, Junior was three, Sister was two and she was expecting my brother Bob in April. Daddy talked her into it, saying it would be good for me and, besides, maybe less work for her. Maybe he was right. Just for a few weeks.

Mother said she stood in the yard and watched the car drive away, a knot in her stomach. I remember looking out the back window of the car and seeing her standing there, one arm under an apron, waving a white dish-

cloth at us. The car left a dust cloud and I couldn't see her anymore.

Little did I know that it would be more than four months before I saw my mother again.

We drove into Browns-ville in the middle of the night, or in the wee hours of the morning. We went into a very nice house. Aunt Gladys took me into the back bedroom, where there was a large four-poster bed with clean-smelling sheets. The room seemed so large.

She got me ready and helped me up into the bed. I was scared and lonely. I had always slept with my brother and sisters, all in one bed. Now I had to sleep alone. She turned out the light and left the room. I began to cry. The sobs and wailing went on a long time. It was so dark and lonely. I wanted my family. No amount of consoling would quiet me, so finally she got a paddle and whipped me. I cried myself to sleep that night, but I never cried again. I can't remember what she told me to get me not to.

Soon I became a part of her life. Aunt Gladys ran a kindergarten and day care in Brownsville and had children coming every morning, five days a week. We had

Aunt Gladys, who became Sister Agatha Linn.

snacks and juices, homemade orange and grapefruit juice from her citrus trees in back and grape juice, which I had never had before. She gave dance lessons in the afternoons and I took them, practicing before the large mirrors that lined one side of the room.

We took trips to Mexico and to the beach. She dressed me up in fancy clothes and showed me around to all her friends, acting like I was her little girl. I wore beautiful dresses and shoes. But she was not a very affectionate woman. She seldom hugged me or gave me a kiss. She did bring me a white rabbit, which I kept in a cage in the back yard and fed every day. I had everything I wanted.

Every Sunday we went to Mass at the Catholic Church. I also went to Sunday school there. Even now when I smell incense I remember the smell in the big dark church, where the priests would swing the incense back and forth and I wondered what on earth they were doing. I huddled next to Aunt Gladys, afraid they were going to hit me with their swaying lanterns or whatever they were. The nuns scared me, too. I didn't like going to that church, but I had to, and I did like being with the other little kids in the class.

As the weeks went by I dreamed of Mother and Daddy often and sometimes woke up with nightmares. I wondered what they were all doing. Thanksgiving came and went and December came.

When Aunt Gladys didn't bring me back home in the three weeks she'd promised, my mother wrote a letter telling her to bring me home. Aunt Gladys wrote back and said she had decided not to bring me back and that she wanted to adopt me. She told them that she could give me a much better home than they could. They were so poor and had four children and another on the way, so one less child would help a lot. She told Mother she would make a good mother and give me the life they couldn't give me.

When Mother read the rest of the letter, she later told me, she became so angry she began to cry. Gladys had written, "You and Lawrence are terrible to be bringing so many children in this world and not have any money, and I am helping you out!"

Mother didn't know what to do. She had no phone or money for long-distance calls. Finally she wrote a letter telling her sister-in-law if she did not send me home soon she was going to the sheriff and would have her arrested for kidnapping. Mother was also angry with Daddy because he was just letting her handle it, and didn't seem concerned that I was not there.

Mother just knew I would be home for Christmas. She was able to scrape up enough money to buy toys, and dolls for the girls. Christmas passed and I still wasn't home. But Gladys sent word she would be at McCoy on New Year's Day.

I had Christmas in Brownsville with Aunt Gladys and her boyfriend, who I was supposed to call Uncle Clarence. I had lots of toys, including a beautiful Shirley Temple doll with a beautiful wicker doll carriage.

On New Year's Day she took me to McCoy, where Highway 281 met the road to our farm. Daddy met us there, I got in his old model A and Aunt Gladys drove on to San Antonio. We drove the long, winding dirt road to the farm.

My mother, sisters and brother were waiting in the yard as we drove up. It was a cold winter day. I could see the smoke from the woodstove coming out of the stovepipe in the roof. We may have had no electricity or plumbing, but it was home.

Everyone gathered around me. Mother gathered me up in her arms and hugged me, and we all went into the house. I showed them my Shirley Temple doll and the wicker buggy, the only toys Aunt Gladys let me take home. I didn't bring many clothes, either. The girls oohed over the doll and I let them hold her. Then Mother reached up on top of the tall chifferobe we had and brought down a beautiful little baby doll. I loved it. I clutched it to my chest and hugged it. It felt so good. It became my favorite doll. I smelled the latex face and felt the soft body of the doll and felt so secure.

After unloading my suitcase, Daddy came in and said, "Bertie Lee, Gladys said for me to have Lois at the McCoy station on Monday and she will pick her up to take her back home with her."

Mother looked at him, startled. "What did you tell her?"

He said, "I said, Okay, I would."

Mother looked at him hard and didn't say a word. She walked into the other room, grabbed me and hugged me so hard I couldn't breathe. I remember the tears coming down her cheeks onto my arms and legs. Finally she loosened her hold and told me to run play with the other kids.

The subject was never mentioned again. When Monday came not a word was said. Daddy went out to do the chores. Mother worked around the house and cooked and cleaned. Daddy didn't go to McCoy. I don't know how long Gladys waited before she knew he wasn't coming.

It took my mother a long time to forgive Aunt Gladys, who never thought she had done anything wrong. It also took my mother a long time to forgive my father for not standing up to his sister.

When my brother Bob was born in April, Aunt Gladys wrote Mother another letter, this time telling her she was going to try to adopt her new baby boy. She said, "I am going to take him off your hands and raise him right."

Mother never told me the whole content of the letter, but the things Aunt Gladys wrote in the letter were so hurtful that she was years forgetting and forgiving— partly because she saved the letter. When her heart began to soften toward Aunt Gladys, she would take out the letter and reread it.

Years later Gladys joined a convent. She became Sister Agatha Linn and moved to San Antonio. She and my mother became friends. Mother and Daddy would go visit her sometimes. She came to visit them, always bringing her friend. She came to all the family reunions. When Mother and Daddy moved to San Antonio in the '50s Gladys would come visit them, just to drink coffee, laugh and talk.

Sister Agatha Linn died of cancer in a hospital in San Antonio in the '70s. Toward the end, when she was very sick, she wanted only Mother to come visit. When the nurses called to say that Sister Agatha wanted to see her, Mother dropped what she was doing and went to hold her hand and talk with her.

I once asked Mother how she came to forgive Aunt Gladys. She said it was when she finally threw that letter away and could forget the past.

6. Christmas on the Farm

We decorated our Christmas tree on Christmas Eve afternoon. It was a tradition. We rushed to do all the chores early. The little tree sat on a library table in front of the window waiting for the homemade decorations and tiny candles.

Our little house was always cold in the winter. We only had a wood cook stove and a wood-burning heater to heat the house. We had to wear several layers of clothing in the house, and sometimes our coats, too.

We didn't have any money, but Daddy worked extra for someone in order to get a small Christmas tree in Floresville, and maybe presents, too. Growing up, we never did know how our parents managed to do Christmas. We just knew there had to be a Santa Claus.

Most of the time we made all our decorations, like cranberry and popcorn strings, colored paper chains and stars made from bright construction paper. Mother had little clips on the tree for candles and some shiny silver tinsel rope that was very old. Sometimes we collected bits of tinfoil we found from gum and things like that to make ornaments that shone and reflected the light of the candles on the tree. We saved icicles from the tree to use again the next year.

Finally the tree was finished. Mother found a match to light the candles. It was always the most beautiful tree I ever saw. With only a kerosene lamp in the room for light, the tree glowed and sparkled like a mirage. We all sat transfixed, not saying a word.

Somehow Mother and Daddy always seemed to come up with one gift apiece for us. The girls got baby dolls and the boys got a little truck or a ball or a cowboy pistol. We all got a big rubber ball to share. It wasn't much, but we kids knew the gifts had to have been from Santa Claus since it was common knowledge around our house that our parents didn't have the money for those kinds of extravagances.

After I was married and had children of my own, I missed Christmas on the farm with my family, even though there were fun times after Eddie and I married because the Wauson family was so compatible.

We had decorating parties weeks before Christmas. All the family came to our little garage apartment to help decorate the tree. We had eggnog, wine coolers, cookies, Mom Wauson's fruitcakes, hot coffee and chocolate. Fifty years later there is still a Wauson Christmas party the week before Christmas, even though we haven't been in years.

When my kids came along and we started our own traditions there were more happy times, like Christmas Eve services and coming home to open one gift before bedtime, reading *The Night Before Christmas*, the children hearing the sound of bells outside their windows (their daddy with some sleigh bells), Christmas morning and the trip to one of the grandmas' houses for Christmas dinner in the afternoon.

We alternated years with our families, but when Mother and Daddy moved to San Antonio in 1957, we tried to see both families on the same day.

There seemed to be sad times, too, at Christmas. The first really sad Christmas was the year Eddie's sister Helen lost her husband on Christmas night. He was only 31 years old, but he had heart problems and pneumonia. He left her and four small children. We were all at the hospital that Christmas. That tragedy stayed in our memory for years. I know it did for Helen.

As the years went by, the really happy Christmases became fewer and farther between. I kept trying to grasp the feeling and emotions of my childhood Christmases, but the holiday was no longer a simple, beautiful time to be with family. It was so commercialized and busy.

When my children got older, I tried to change the way I felt by doing something for someone. I took Kristi and Derek shopping and we bought presents for a little boy and girl. I took the kids out to the Lena Pope Children's Home to meet two children, who they "adopted" and gave presents in their rooms. The kids loved it, my kids and the ones at the home. But I left sad, because I really wanted to take them home with me and not leave them there.

Sometimes I still want to put a plate of cookies by the tree and eat them before I go to bed, leaving a few crumbs, just to pretend. I still get goose bumps when I hear "O Holy Night" and "Silent Night," and I still like to listen to Andy Williams sing all those wonderful carols.

When I see the elaborate lights and decorations around the city at night, I feel so nostalgic. My heart aches for the times when Christmas was so simple, and the most wonderful things we had were our imagination and the love of our family.

I stand out in my front yard, look up into the sky and see that bright star in the East. I smile to myself. It is still the same star that the angels saw over 2,000 years ago, when Jesus Christ was born. It is the same star I saw in 1939. The night is cold, the sky is black, the stars are so bright, especially that one.

I am again seven years old. I can hear the cows lowing down in the pen, the howl of a lone coyote far off, and Mother calling me to come in because the girls are waiting for me to get in bed with them so we can all stay warm. I can smell the coffee on the back of the old woodstove and the aroma of cookies baking.

I shiver with the excitement of Christmas Eve, take one last look at the star and run back into the house.

7. Starting School

August in South Texas is usually hot, dry and depressing, the "dog days" of summer. By then we were ready for school to start. Truthfully, I never wanted school to be out. But we still had several more weeks of picking corn, hauling hay or sometimes, if the planting was early enough, peanut thrashing to be done.

The first day of school was still two weeks away. The temperature was reaching the century mark and the hot sand blew off the field near the house and across our yard. Two weeks seemed so far off.

At night when it was so hot, we went down to the tank in the pasture to take a dip in the murky cool water. The marshy smell of the tank water filled my nostrils. I liked listening to the frogs croaking in the night. They could almost put me to sleep, but the fear of water moccasins kept me on my toes.

Once, feeling something slithering by me in the water, I jumped out, hollering, "It's time to go back to the house." We dried off and went up to the house and went to bed as the breeze came up from the south, and I drifted to sleep thinking about the first day of school.

Before school started, Mother made out her order from the Sears, Roebuck catalog. We hung over her shoulder as she filled out the form in the light of the kerosene lamp: "four pairs of oxford shoes, brown." Then she measured our feet with a piece of cardboard, sending along with the order four perfectly cut out feet for our shoe sizes.

Then there were orders for socks, underwear, one ready-made dress for each of us girls and pants for the boys. She picked out some pretty flowered, checkered and

Kasper students, from left, top row, Matilda Valcher, James Meyer, Willia Pearl Kasper, Kenneth Raabe, Henrietta Pundt, Sam Meyer and Eileen Schultz; front row, Floyd Raabe, Margie Mergele, Billy Haese, Margaret Kolodziej, Ima Lee Gloor, Alphonse Theis and Ruby Valcher.

plaid material to make dresses for us and shirts for the boys, along with all the feed sacks she'd washed and saved through the summer to make more dresses and shirts.

When the order came and she opened it, we were as excited as if it were Christmas. Sure enough, all the shoes fit perfectly. Now there was one week until school started.

School didn't start until after Labor Day back then. That Saturday, Mother and Daddy went into town to Floresville to the C & C Dime Store or to J. C. Merchant's Store for school supplies. We tagged along with Mother as she bought the Big Chief tablets, bright yellow pencils, writing books, crayons, rulers, scissors and composition notebooks. Oh, the smell of a Big Chief Tablet! When we got home, I put my supplies under my pillow so I could go to sleep with the sweet smell of the tablet and pencils.

Finally Labor Day came, then Tuesday, the first day of school. Usually the heat wave had finally broken with a thunderstorm crashing across the Tardia Hills. Mother walked us up the sandy road. Carrying my Big Chief tab-

HENRIETTA PUNDT ARNOLD

let and pencil, wearing my new brown oxford shoes and my new dress made from feed sacks, I felt like a princess.

I couldn't wait to get my new books. The readers were my favorite, although I loved the geography books. As she entered first grade, I knew my sister Elizabeth would love her Dick and Jane reader.

For a special treat Mother let us bring our lunch, like everyone else. She put it in a bright shiny syrup bucket, with a lid on it and shiny handles. Inside we had a fried-egg sandwich and a piece of cornbread, with butter and syrup between the halves.

On the back porch of the Kasper School, near the well where the boys would draw water every morning and fill the big coolers on the bench, there was a long row of nails with tin cups hanging on them, one for each of us.

Mother took us to our assigned desks, kissed us good-bye and went back home. Now came the good part, passing out the textbooks. I was ready for another school year.

September to me still means starting school. And I still love the smell of Big Chief Tablets.

One of my teachers, Miss Johnie Carnes, with her niece, Patricia Poth, beside the school.

8. Winter Days at Kasper School

You could hear the north wind blowing, whistling through the trees and around the windows in the three-room schoolhouse we sat in that morning. I think it must have been about 1940. It was January and very cold.

Kasper School was a large school compared to most country schools; some only had one room. Near the school was even a "teacherage," which is what they called the house the teacher lived in.

Most students walked to school, some for miles. Since we lived only a quarter of a mile away down a country lane, we always came, no matter what the weather, even though the roads were wet, muddy and icy from the rain and sleet. Not many cars ventured down the road in this kind of weather.

The temperature had dropped during the night when the cold, wet norther blew in. It was near 25 degrees outside and not much warmer inside. Once in a while I could hear the sound of sleet hitting the windows. Of the few students who came that day, the older ones grouped around the potbellied iron stove and the younger ones were told to take out their arithmetic books.

Our teachers, Mr. and Mrs. Poth, got there early to get the fire started. They continued to stoke the fire and add more wood. I could feel the heat on my face even as my back was freezing. We all kept our coats on to help keep warm. When we finally got warm enough, we dragged benches near the stove and sat there to have our lessons.

The older kids were to keep busy reading or doing some kind of busy work while we waited for our turn for a class. There were only my sisters and brother and me—Margaret, Sister and Junior—and Ruby Lee Valchar, who also lived close enough to walk in the cold rain.

Alphonse Theis and LeRoy Schneider and Billy Haese were there because their parents always brought them in cars when they couldn't ride their bikes or horses. I thought those boys were rich because they were the only kids in school who owned bicycles. They lived several miles away but could ride them to school on nice days.

The Ximenez boys could have come to school because they lived so close, but they used any excuse to not come. My brothers envied them because they were very independent, daring and fun to be around. It was rumored they even smoked and sometimes let their little six-year-old brother have a puff.

I liked it when they came to school and we could trade our lunches for theirs. They would have stuff like tortillas wrapped around a piece of fried rabbit. We would trade our ham or cheese on homemade bread for that any day! But they didn't come that day.

We spent the morning doing reading, writing, arithmetic, geography and health. The morning went fast, especially when our teachers made us all cocoa. We didn't have recess because it was too cold. If we needed to go to the outhouse, we had a ten-minute break, and the boys headed for their outhouse and the girls to theirs. It was so cold as we battled the wind and sleet to get there. To sit on that cold wooden seat was awful. Sometimes I just waited till I got home and could go to our own cold outhouse.

At noon, Mrs. Poth said it was time to go home. School was over for the day.

I loved Mrs. Poth. She emphasized reading and encouraged us to get books from the bookmobile that came every two weeks, books like the Bobbsey Twins series and Nancy Drew mysteries. In fact, she made the ones who didn't like to read get books anyway. We were to put them on the shelf when we were finished and then we could read what we wanted of all the others. I would read ten or twenty books in two weeks.

That day I went over to the bookshelf to see what I could take home to read. I saw something called *Black Beauty*. It looked hard, but I decided I'd try it. Mother and Daddy would help me with the big words. I let Mrs. Poth check it out for me as we gathered our books and put our scarves around our heads to walk home.

Margaret, Junior, Sister and I started down the road to our house. Since we were facing north, the cold sleet kept hitting us in the face, stinging as it hit our bare legs and hands. We tucked our hands inside our coats with our books, and tried to walk.

They took off running, but I turned and walked backwards to be warmer. I could see the white schoolhouse receding in the distance, a curl of smoke from the stove still circling above the roof. When I could no longer see the schoolhouse, I turned and ran in the sleet and rain until I came to our house, where smoke was also coming from its stovepipe.

I can still see every room in the school, along with the desks, closets, bookshelves and books. To this day I love the smell of chalk, freshly sharpened pencils and Big Chief Tablets. And when I hear sleet hitting the windows, I think of Kasper School.

9. My Eighth Birthday

It was my eighth birthday. I was very excited, not because of my birthday but because I was going to a real birthday party. It wasn't my party, but I didn't care. Billy Haese had the same birthday I did, March 11. He was having a big party at his grandfather's dairy farm and had invited all the kids from school.

I had read about birthday parties in books, but we had never had one or even been to one. Of course we usually had a cake with candles for our birthdays, and with lots of brothers and sisters around that probably was like a party. I don't remember presents, probably because there wasn't enough money for luxuries like that. But this was different.

My teacher, Johnie Carnes, took us kids over to the farm. I can still see the view from the gate, the lawn decorated with balloons and streamers. I can't remember much about the party except for the luscious cake and ice cream and the long tables covered with tablecloths and cake and presents. We played games like Drop the Handkerchief and Pin the Tail on the Donkey. As Billy opened his presents, my eyes bugged out of my head to see so many. I felt like I was in a dream.

When the party was over, Miss Carnes took us back to the school. Margaret and Junior started toward the lane to our house. Miss Carnes called me back into the "teacherage," where her sister and brother-in-law, the teachers and principal, lived. I waited in their sitting room as she went to the other room.

She came back and handed me a beautiful birthday present, wrapped in pretty paper and a ribbon. She said,

"This is your present. I know today is your birthday, too." I carefully removed the pretty paper so I wouldn't tear it, and there was my present, a book, *Bobbsey Twins in the Country*. It was the first book I ever owned, and I treasured it for many years.

After that I read every book in the Bobbsey Twins series. Then I went on to read all the books in the Nancy Drew series, the Hardy Boys series and the Grace Livingston Hill books. Then Zane Gray became my favorite author, and I read all his books. I read the San Antonio *Light*, which came every day to our mailbox.

For the last sixty-plus years I probably have read thousands of books, and my library is extensive. I owe it all to Alfreda Poth, who taught me to read, and to Johnie Carnes, who gave me a love for books and the gift of that one special book on my eighth birthday.

10. Summer Days in the Country

Summer time these days means things like no school, going to the pool or the mall, hanging out in the sun, getting a tan, taking a vacation, playing baseball, skateboarding all day, going to movie matinees and all those fun things kids look forward to when school is out.

In my youth and teen years, our summers were spent working in the fields once we were old enough to hold a hoe to chop weeds and grass out of the peanuts or watermelons, or old enough to reach the cornstalks to pull corn and throw it into a wagon bed.

Being the oldest, I always worked in the fields. Margaret worked sometimes, but most of the time she was the one to stay home and help Mother with housecleaning, cooking and washing. I still think it is because she wanted to listen to "Stella Dallas" on the battery radio, or maybe "One Man's Family," or any of those radio soaps popular back in the '40s. But, being athletic or a tomboy and loving the outdoors so much, I really didn't mind. I just learned to work as hard as my brothers.

When our school at Kasper let out at the end of May, I dreaded the days to come. After we woke at sunup, we went out to slop the hogs, milk the cows, feed the chickens, let the cows out in the pasture for the day, pen up the calves and head for the house with the milk. We'd eat our breakfast of oatmeal and maybe biscuits, then put on our straw hats and take off for the fields, carrying our hoes.

As the sun rose higher and grew hotter, we worked through the morning, up one row and down another and back to the end of the row to get a drink of cool water from the water bag hanging in the shade of a tree. Then it

Taking a break on a summer day: Lawrence Jr., Margaret, Lois (holding baby Gerry), Elizabeth and Babe.

was back up another row, intermingled with bouts of dirt clod fights and a lot of teasing and fighting between the boys and the girls. I could always throw as hard as the boys and my aim was pretty good, so our brothers pretty much didn't mess with us girls.

We didn't have a clock with us, but we watched the overhead sun, and when it was straight up it was time to go to lunch, though we called it dinner. We headed for the house for a cheese sandwich on homemade bread, or maybe macaroni with tomato sauce, which Mother would cook for us if we were lucky.

We'd lie down and rest for maybe 30 minutes or an hour, though if Daddy was anywhere around it would be much shorter. He didn't like us kids lying around much. If he came driving up in his truck, we hurriedly got up, put on our shoes and headed out the screen door, acting like we had just come in. We didn't want to be yelled at.

We spent the afternoon in the same monotonous routine, row after row of chopping weeds and grass. As the afternoon dragged on the sun finally seemed to be lowering. When it was almost to the horizon we knew it was time to go home, call in the cows and start milking. The younger ones were to feed the chickens and hogs and gather eggs.

By 9 p.m. we finally ate supper and were so exhausted we could barely walk down to the windmill once the wind kicked up some, enough to whirl the blades around enough for a stream of water to come up out of the pipe in the ground. The pipe was about five feet, high just about high enough for us to get under and have a "shower." We girls would bathe first and get dressed for bed, then the boys would come down and take their turns.

Falling into bed we'd try to sleep, even though there was not much breeze through the old windows of our frame house, nor insulation. Tossing and turning as beads of sweat ran off us, we often finally got up, took the sheets and set up a cot outside to sleep under the stars. A breeze would waft across us finally. I remember dropping off as I stared up at the Milky Way and all the millions of stars, wondering if there was a future for me other than this.

I had read in many books of far-off places, cities and towns of beauty, green forests, green lawns, people sitting in pretty houses having fancy dinners, living a type of life I could only read about and dream of. Things would be different and I would be different. I wasn't going to spend my whole life chopping weeds out of peanuts or milking cows!

The next morning, the same dreary, hard day would come again. We had to work six days a week, sometimes seven if it was harvest time.

When September came and school started, I would be seeing people besides my family. There'd be my teachers, whom I loved and respected, and the wonderful books and learning, and school was also our social life.

Summer in the country was not exactly a fun time for farm children, but you do learn a lot of good values. Maybe it made me appreciate having some leisure time, and such things as vacations. I don't think farm kids know the meaning of "lazy." We never got a chance to learn. And for that I thank God and my parents.

11. Bertie Lee's Best Year

It was 1930. He had a fancy new car, a Model A coupe with one of those "mother-in-law" seats in the back. My mother, Bertie Lee Goode, was 18. She was on a double date with one of her good friends who was with her boyfriend and her friend's brother, recently divorced.

Mother's date was the young divorced man. He was the one with the brand new car. Not many people had new cars in 1930. Her father let her go because he thought he was a nice guy. They parked near the river bridge and her friend and her boyfriend went walking down the road to go across the bridge.

As my mother told me this story, she laughed as she said, a little wickedly, "Well, he began to get rough with me, so I said, 'If you touch me, I'm gonna kick out the windshield of this car.' Now he was proud of that car—it was a brand new car, you know. He jumped out of the car and yelled for his sister. He told her to get back up there 'cause he was ready to go home. And home we went!"

She said she never had any more trouble with the boys in town after that.

Bertie Lee was a fun person. She loved to dance and hang around with her friends. They all smoked, and probably even drank bootleg alcohol. "The Jenkins and the Laramores, those were my good friends," she said.

"We lived in Coleman County then. We had lots of fun. We ran around together for years. I had a boyfriend later on that year. His name was Stroud Jenkins. I was crazy about him. We went out all the time. If there was a new movie in town, he took me to that. We were together all summer."

But by the end of the summer Stroud got a job in Waxahachie and moved away. He and Bertie Lee got engaged, and he was going to send for her later on. Then her daddy decided to go to South Texas to Wilson County, because there was good cotton picking there. His brother was picking cotton near Floresville and convinced Earl to come down for a couple of months.

Bertie Lee in 1930.

"I didn't want to leave," Mother said. "All my friends were in Coleman. My cousins were all there, too. But we had to go. We went down to pick cotton and make some money. I was feeling like my life was all shot. Here I was 18 years old and I had to go down and pick cotton with a bunch of people I didn't even know. My boyfriend had just moved away. I was leaving all my cousins and friends. I felt real bad!

"When we got down to Floresville, we met these people, a nice old German family, and they had a couple of boys and me and William, my brother, met them and began to run around with them. They invited us to parties and dances. We picked cotton, but we started to have some fun, too, with the Mann boys. We would go over to Three Oaks to all the dances. It was a lot of fun.

"After a couple of months, Mr. Mann talked my daddy into staying there, so he got a truck and went with him back to Coleman to get all our stuff and he started looking for us a place to rent near his place. Later on he found us a place up there close to the old Zook place and we moved in there."

I asked her what happened to Stroud Jenkins, and she said, "I don't know what happened. We lost contact with each other. I guess he started going out with other girls and I was having fun, too. I really did like him, though."

That was a cold, hard winter. Her mother and daddy were struggling to survive and put food on the table for their large family. Earl was going to plant a crop in the spring on the Mann place. Bertie Lee worked hard, as she was the oldest and was a big help to her mother, who was expecting a baby again—her eleventh child, eight of them living. Bertie Lee yearned for some kind of freedom from the drudgery and life of a farmer's wife.

Right after Christmas, her brother William told her that a neighbor, Lawrence Zook, who he had gotten to be friends with, wanted him to go to a New Year's Eve Dance over at Three Oaks, and wondered if his sister wanted to go. She wasn't interested in Lawrence—he was 10 years older than her, and she had called him that "hog farmer down the road"—but she wanted to go to the dance, and jumped at the chance. That night she fell in love again.

From that night on her life changed. Lawrence started courting her, and by the next May they were married. She moved down the road to the Zook farm, but never left the life of drudgery. For 26 years she and Daddy lived on the farm and raised eight children.

After struggling for so many years fighting undependable weather, they finally gave up farming and in 1957 moved to San Antonio, where she had a good job with the San Antonio State Hospital and retired many years later. Life became easier when Daddy went to work as a night watchman for a steel company. They had regular paychecks!

After Daddy died in 1984, she moved into a retirement apartment complex and had many friends. When they would have dances down in the social and dining hall, Bertie Lee was the one who did most of the dancing.

She was in her 70s but was the best dancer there. The men lined up to dance with her.

That summer of 1930 was the last carefree time my mother had. When she talked about it that night, at age 75, her eyes softened. She remembered the parties, the dances and picnics, swimming in the river, the movies and being in love.

She said, "That was the best year of my life, I think."

12. The Day I Ran Away From Home

That day in October 1944, started off warm and still, very warm for an October Saturday. It was Saturday, but we weren't going to town. Not enough money to buy groceries. Everyone was in a bad mood. I was 12, and it was a very bad day for me.

I can't remember if Mother was not in a good mood because Daddy had yelled at her about something before he left to work in the fields, or if I was fighting with my sisters about something. All I know was it seemed like everyone was against me. I got yelled at for no reason. I even got a spanking. Mother didn't spank us often, but if she did, it was with a peach tree switch, which we had to go and get ourselves.

My legs were red and stinging. I ran out of the house crying. It wasn't my fault. It was never my fault, of course. I felt so abused. I walked down to the barn and out toward the pasture, thinking and crying. I stepped in a pile of chicken manure, which made it even worse. I had to stop, scrape it off my foot and wipe my foot in the hay behind the barn.

I opened the barn door and went in, sniffing the cool, musty smell of the hay and corn. Looking around for spiders and bugs and maybe even a snake, I crawled behind the pile of corn. I lay there thinking about my bad morning and began to cry even more, engulfed by self-pity.

I knew my brothers and sisters were still at the house finishing breakfast, helping clear the table and doing the dishes. I could hear them as they came out to play.

I decided to stay there and figure out what to do.

A couple of hours went by. I dozed a while, then began to make plans. I'd show them! I'll make them think I had run away from home. They'd think I was lost in the big pasture next to our farm. They'd all come looking for me, calling, "Lois, Lois, where are you?" Mother would be crying, feeling really bad that she spanked me and yelled at me.

The day dragged by, but no one came looking. I heard my brothers and sisters hollering and laughing in a game of cops and robbers. I knew a Texas norther had come in, because I could hear the wind blowing through the cracks in the barn. It began to get cooler behind that pile of corn.

I knew it was past noon because my stomach began to rumble. Still no one came looking for me. I kept listening for the barn door to open. I thought Mother, sad and worried, had gone into town to get the sheriff to help look. I nestled down in the corn, enjoying my daydream, and fell asleep.

When I awoke there were deep shadows in the barn. I could hear Margaret and Junior in the pen next to the barn, doing the milking, were laughing and talking. Someone came into the stalls next to me, gathering eggs from the nests. It sounded like Sister and Bubber. They weren't even talking about me. No one seemed to be missing me.

I heard the tractor and knew Daddy was coming in from the fields. I waited. Things got quieter. Darkness moved in. I got up from my hiding place and crept to the door, opened it a crack and peaked out. No sign of anyone. I could see the shadow of the tractor against the sky where the sun had gone down. There was a faint glow coming from the window at the house, and I knew they were getting ready to sit down for supper.

I stepped out of the barn and began to walk slowly toward the house. I stood under the big gnarled mesquite tree by the smokehouse and watched.

As I got near the kitchen window, I could see inside. Everyone was gathered around the big table with the two long benches on each side, all the kids lined up eating, laughing and talking. Mother was passing around her freshly -baked rolls, and Daddy was pouring syrup in his plate along with a huge pat of butter.

My mouth was watering. I was so hungry and thirsty. I was chilled by the cold wind coming in from the north, and shivered as I watched them drink their big glasses of milk. I wanted to be there so bad. But no one had missed me! What should I do?

Finally, I gave in and walked around to the front porch and came through the front door. Without a word, I walked to the table and found my place at the end of the bench. Margaret scooted over so I could sit down. Mother handed me a plate with some rolls and butter and syrup, and poured me a glass of milk from the big earthen pitcher.

Everyone just kept on talking and laughing. They acted like I had never been gone. It was as if I had been there all day. I pretended I had been there, too.

The incident was never mentioned. I never asked why no one had looked for me. I think maybe I was afraid they would say they hadn't missed me. Were my brothers and sisters happy I wasn't there to boss them around? Did Mother not miss me, with so many kids around? Or did she see me go into the barn and tell the rest of the family to ignore me? She knew I would come home? I think it was the last reason.

I never ran away again.

13. The Arcadia Theatre

I'll never forget going to the Arcadia Theatre in Floresville on Saturday afternoons. We somehow always came up with a dime or a quarter to see the movies. The smell of popcorn and the cool, air-conditioning inside were things I looked forward to whenever Mother and Daddy would take us to town.

Back in the '40s there was Melba Stevens handing out tickets in the booth, with a smile that promised a whole new world inside to a bunch of kids from the country.

Of course, they showed westerns at the Saturday matinees, usually a double feature. I loved Hopalong Cassidy, Roy Rogers, Gene Autry and Charles Starrett. Margaret had a crush on Roy Rogers. I had a crush on all of them.

Maybe that's when I began to daydream about a tall, handsome cowboy carrying me off on his horse into the western plains. For hours I could forget the hard work on the farm. I could forget my one pair of shoes that had to last all year. I could pretend I was Dale Evans.

I began to keep scrapbooks of movie stars. If I had some extra money I would buy *Movie Screen* or magazines like that and cut out the pictures of Jennifer Jones and Robert Cotton, Claudette Colbert and Maureen O'Hara, along with Clark Gable and other handsome stars.

It was at the movies that we saw the carnage of World War II, in newsreels between features. Reading about the war in the newspaper was bad enough, but seeing the newsreels made me realize how scary war was. I watched the rallies for War Bonds and the big picture of Uncle Sam, pointing his finger at me, saying, "America Needs You." War seemed so near.

When the war with the Japanese ended in 1945, Mother and Daddy took the day off and went to the Arcadia to see "Song of Bernadette," with Jennifer Jones and Joseph Cotton. We waited excitedly for them to come home that night so they could tell us all about it. We sat at the big dinner table covered with a faded oilcloth and they told us all the beautiful story.

14. Daddy Was a Democrat

Election Day in South Texas was one of the most exciting days in our lives. Daddy was into politics. He could talk about his favorite candidate for hours, if anyone was around to listen. That is pretty much what we did—listen; Mother, too. Daddy loved politics almost as much as he loved farming. We couldn't get a word in edgewise.

Daddy had been a Democrat as long as I could remember. He thought Franklin Roosevelt hung the moon, and Harry Truman was his kind of man—tough talking, straight shooting, letting out a cuss word once in a while. I think Daddy only voted Republican once in his life. That was for Richard Nixon, something he always regretted.

Politics in Wilson County was rough and tough during the '30s and '40s. Sam Fore, publisher of the Floresville *Chronicle-Journal*, was a big factor in getting so many men elected. He had lots of influence and helped get Lyndon Johnson elected to the Senate. If Sam Fore and the *Chronicle-Journal* endorsed a candidate, you could almost bet he would win. If the man was good enough for Sam Fore, he was good enough for Daddy.

Daddy ran for office only once in his life and that was for the Kasper school board. He won, too, and served for many years. I guess everyone figured he knew what he was talking about since he had eight kids.

Daddy was on the school board in 1948 when they had to hire a new teacher. When he came home from the board meeting that night I heard him telling Mother about how they had interviewed a man from San Antonio for the job. He really liked the man. But, he said, "I don't know about that wife of his."

"Why?" asked Mother. "What was she like?"

Daddy said, "Oh, she's purty young. She's just a flip of a girl."

We laughed at that for years, because the board hired that man, Richard Wauson, and his little "flip of a wife" and little boy moved into the house next to the school. The couple became good friends to Mother and Daddy. They would play cards and dominoes together, and Lessie became my mother's best friend. That is how I met my husband, Eddie, Richard's brother.

Daddy loved election days. We all did. He called it "sitting on the box." No matter if it was a local, school, state or national election, Daddy and Mother both looked forward to the day. Sometimes Mother would work the polls, as they called it. Daddy would even take the day off from farm work, which very seldom happened. It was a chance to see all the neighbors and catch up on the news in Wilson County.

When Daddy came home after the polls closed and they had counted the boxes, we would listen to the news and stories, then go to bed as he and Mother sat up late listening to our battery-operated radio, before rural electrification came through. They would listen late into the night.

If Daddy's man lost, he would be in a bad mood and talk to himself and cuss under his breath for days. If his man won, he was in a good mood, because he hoped for higher farm prices and help for the farmer.

When I married Eddie, I found he and his brothers also loved politics and were Democrats, so he fit right into my family. Eddie and Daddy would talk politics for hours, with Daddy doing most of the talking and Eddie listening.

It was while we were engaged in 1950 that Eddie and I got into an argument one night about Truman firing General MacArthur. I was on one side, and he was on the other. The argument got so heated it almost caused us to break our engagement.

I found out how serious my husband was about election days in 1952. We were expecting our first baby. Eddie took me to the hospital early in the morning on Tuesday, November 4. I was in labor all day and still had not delivered when it was getting time for the polls to close. He had not yet gone to vote and began to get nervous, because he wanted to vote for Adlai Stevenson. By 6 p.m. my pains were getting very close together, but he said, "Honey, I am going to go vote. I will be back as soon as I can."

I stared at him, scared, because this was my first baby and I wanted my husband there. I said, "What if the baby comes before you get back?"

He said, "I promise I will come back real fast. Nothing will happen till I get back." He left to go vote.

While he was gone, my contractions got closer and harder. I kept looking at the clock in the labor room. It was after 7. Suddenly he walked through the door, grinning. "See? I made it back!" he said.

The baby was born around 8, and everything was fine. Eddie left the hospital later, as I drifted off to sleep, to go home and listen to the election results. I didn't care who won. I was glad the birth was over, and I had my baby boy.

The next morning Eddie came to the hospital, discouraged. He had bad news. Adlai Stevenson had lost to Dwight Eisenhower.

I said, "See, your vote didn't help that man at all!"

I shouldn't have rubbed it in. It was a sad time for the Zooks and the Wausons as far as Election Day went, but we had something more wonderful to celebrate—our first baby boy, Eddie Trent Wauson. It was a pretty good year, election or no election.

15. A Christmas Football

It was Christmas in South Texas. That summer the drought had devastated the crops, and times were hard. Daddy stared at the blue sky all summer long, but there was no rain. The crops withered and died in the fields. Harvest never came.

A blue norther came in the week before Christmas, and the icy wind blew in clouds of dust and sand. It seeped through the cracks in the old house we lived in, and through places in the windowpanes where cardboard covered up the holes. The old iron potbellied stove kept everyone warm if you got close enough to it.

We all knew there wasn't going to be any Christmas that year. We'd heard Mother and Daddy talking in the night and knew there was no money for gifts or even a tree. All my brothers and sisters went on doing their chores—feeding the chickens and hogs, milking the cows and thinking about Christmas a few days away.

Mother managed to buy a little tree that year with some money from selling eggs in town. The tree got decorated on Christmas Eve, with all the old ornaments and homemade paper chains, popcorn and cranberries.

My brother Bob was about 14. He loved football and had wanted a football for months. He'd been hoping to get one for Christmas, and it was all he dreamed and talked about. "I went to bed that night," Bob told us years later, "just thinking about all those years when I used to believe in Santa and just knew he was going to come, landing on the roof and coming in and leaving all us kids a gift and maybe some candies and apples and oranges and nuts.

"But I was too old, and I knew better. I knew that when I woke in the morning there would be no football."

The next morning all of the kids got up and ran to look under the tree. Bob walked slowly into the room, not wanting to look. But there it was! Lying under the tree, the most beautiful official NFL football he had ever seen.

Telling us this story 50 years later, tears came to his eyes, his voice choked and he could hardly talk. Then he quietly said, "I was 14 years old, but at that moment I really believed there was a Santa Claus!"

He found out years afterward that just a few days before Christmas, a Christmas card came in the mail from Uncle Everett. In it was a Christmas present, a check. He told Mother to use it for Christmas presents for all the kids.

I wonder if Uncle Everett ever knew that his love and generosity caused a 14-year old boy to believe in miracles.

16. Peanut Threshing

Daddy was a peanut farmer. For many years peanuts were the crop he made his money on, if it rained. We had 100 acres in Wilson County, but only about 60 percent of it was farmed. The rest was in pasture. It was good sandy soil, good for peanuts.

Spring was planting time. If it rained, Daddy would go out and scratch the surface of the ground to see if there were sprouts on the peanut seed. If he saw some he came home happy and whistling or singing. If not, he scowled and cussed under his breath.

As the peanuts began to come up, so did the weeds, Johnson grass and crab grass. That was when us kids were sent to chop the weeds and grass from between the peanut bushes. We called it "chopping peanuts."

As summer went by, if there hadn't been much rain the peanut plants became stunted. My brother Bob—we called him Bubber as we couldn't say "brother"—would follow Daddy out to the edge of the field and stand beside him, helping him watch the horizon for rain clouds.

In a good year the plants were full and thick, with large bunches of peanuts attached underground. Daddy would hang the bushes up on the porch to dry and wait for harvest time.

At threshing time, farmers would take turns going to each farmer's farm, the men and boys sometimes joined by women and teenaged girls. There was usually one threshing machine going around to all the farms.

I looked forward to it with great excitement. One reason was that I had a crush on one boy whose father followed the threshing crews and helped. I was about 12 or

13 and he was a little older. He didn't go to my school but lived in another county. I daydreamed about him for months, but only saw him once in a while in Floresville or at a dance somewhere.

I planned for weeks what I would wear to help Mother to serve lunch—dinner, as we called it—to the workers. Working all morning, we would make more than 100 sandwiches, usually with the bologna Mother had bought in town in long round sticks and sliced real thick. We made thick cheese and salami sandwiches and sometimes peanut butter and jelly sandwiches, too.

While Margaret—"Mogie," as we called her, a holdover from when I couldn't say her name when she was born—and Sister and, later, my sister Gerry, all pitched in to help, I would sneak away to the mirror in Mother's room, to primp and see how my plaid shirt looked with my faded jeans or shorts. I found a piece of lipstick and put some on, hoping Mother wouldn't notice. I could hardly wait to see Richard.

Loading the food along with huge containers of iced tea, homemade cakes and cookies, we went to the field in the pickup. Ice for the tea came from an enormous chunk from the ice house in Floresville and was kept wrapped in thick tow sacks in our wooden icebox.

When we got there, the wagons and flat trailers were coming in piled high with peanuts. Men standing on them were loading the peanut bushes into the threshing machine. I was mesmerized, watching it spit out peanuts into a sack on one side. Women nearby sewed up the sacks with twine.

The peanut leaves and stalks on the other side went into a baler that produced large rectangular bales of peanut hay. That's where I spotted Richard with his father and uncles all working with the bales. I tried not to watch his cute grin and kept busy with my sisters and mother, setting up all the food for the workers.

Finally things came to a halt. The thresher shut down, the hay baler stopped and the men, boys and women came to the wagon where the food and iced tea were laid out. After gathering their food, they hunkered down in the shade of the wagons, tractors or stacks of hay bales, talking and laughing and getting some social time in. I never got near Richard, because he stayed with his cousins and friends. They would look my way sometimes and my heart fluttered, and I would smile and nervously look away.

Finally the day would end and night came over us like a warm blanket. I went to bed listening to the thresher. They had to finish up because the next day they were going on to the next farm.

After a few days, rain came, but Daddy was already happy. Peanut threshing time was over, and the large pile of peanut sacks had been taken to town. The baled hay was covered with a large tarp. On the afternoon of the big rain, Daddy sat on the front porch in his big wooden rocking chair, singing "Old Black Joe." We begged for more songs. He loved to sing "When the Roll Is Called Up Yonder" and other hymns and spirituals.

It had been a good year. And it might be a whole year before I saw Richard again, but that was okay with me. A girl can dream, can't she?

17. Peanut Festival Time

It was Peanut Festival time in Wilson County. Our family looked forward to the festival all year.

The weather in 1947 turned cool late in September. It was Saturday. Mother and Daddy and all of us kids had been up since daybreak. Our chores done, we ate breakfast, got dressed and piled into the Ford pickup to head for town before the parade started.

We needed to get a good parking place in the sandy lot near Merchant's Feed Store beneath one of the big shade trees. The pickup would be our contact point for the day. It was a place to meet, to rest and to bring our friends and talk.

We were early enough to find a parking site under one of the big trees. We kids took off running to get a good place to watch the parade, but my sister Margaret and I tried not to run. We were too old to hang out with the younger kids, so we hung back a little.

Gerry and Donny, the youngest—eight and six—decided to wait for Mother and Daddy. Bubber and Junior—12 and 10—took off to get lost in the crowd. We decided to wait for Sister (Elizabeth), who was 11 and didn't have a sister her age to hang out with.

The three of us walked quickly down the sidewalk, talking excitedly. We had to dodge bunches of peanut bushes over-hanging the eaves above the sidewalk. Both sides of the main street were decorated with peanuts. We could hear the bands warming up across town, and soon the streets were lined with people.

Finally we could see the bands coming, their instruments flashing in the sun. Then came all the honorary chairmen and dignitaries from across Texas. Then the most glamorous part—the floats with the Queen of the Peanut Festival and the Princesses, then the other floats. By the time the last band marched by, the sun was climbing higher in the sky and the smell of hamburgers was wafting from the sidewalk cafe down the street. Grabbing a hamburger and a Coke, we started toward the carnival.

After riding the rides and checking out the booths, we walked back to the dusty lot where our truck was parked. We found Mother sitting in the truck visiting with one of the neighbor women. Daddy was off somewhere having a nonstop conversation with some old cronies, or maybe he was over at the beer joint having a beer. The Peanut Festival was one of the few times he splurged and bought a bottle of Pearl or Lone Star.

We asked Mother if we could go back to the carnival. She said, "Okay, but when it gets dark we will be heading toward home."

Someone I knew was working on one of my favorite rides. His name was Frank, and he went to Poth High School with me. I could tell he was sweet on me. I sort of liked his looks, his cap pushed back off his forehead and his wide grin.

I spent the next two hours on that ride. It began to get dark, and many people were heading home, but I stayed and kept riding. He let me ride for free and I never got off. As I spun high up with the lights of the carnival and the town swirling around me, I felt as if I were in another place, not like a 14-year-old farm girl who lived in an old weathered house with a few broken windows covered with cardboard and no running water. I felt like Cinderella flying off in my fancy coach, with Prince Charming watching me go. I never wanted the night to end.

Suddenly my brother and sisters came running out of the dark shouting, "Lois, you better get to the truck. We've been looking for you. Daddy is mad. We need to go home!"

Frank stopped the ride, and I got off, smiling shyly at him and waving my hand. As I turned the corner, I looked back at him standing in the soft glow of the carnival lights and waving back. It was like stepping out of a dream.

When I got back to the truck the rest of the family was there, waiting. By then Daddy had found someone else to talk to, and he forgot to yell at me. I chose to ride in the back, since I didn't want to be fussed at. I leaned back against the cab, along with Margaret and Sister, and the others lay down on a quilt on the truckbed along with the groceries and chicken feed. Everyone was chattering and talking about their day.

My brothers and sisters teased me some about Frank, but finally everyone was quiet. By the time we got home most of the younger ones were asleep. I had stared at the sky with all the stars blazing in the night and daydreamed about the twirling ride at the carnival. Frank was my Prince Charming, I was Cinderella and I could pretend a little longer.

On Monday, we went back to school. The Peanut Festival seemed so long ago. I saw Frank in the hallway and he looked just like everyone else. He didn't even have his cap on. As I walked past him, I didn't even look his way. He had changed, and so had I. That night at the Peanut Festival was not real—it was my dream world.

But Peanut Festival time would come again. I had a whole year to think about it.

18. My Best Friend

Crystal Warnken had naturally curly hair and a smile that lit up her face. When teenage girls get together they tend to gossip. Not Crystal. She never said a bad word about anyone. I don't think she had one enemy in the whole school. She taught us not to gossip or spread rumors.

She was one of the most beautiful girls I ever met. She never thought she was very pretty, but she was, especially on the inside. She was my role model.

When I entered Poth High School in the fall of 1947, I was just a nervous farm girl excited about being in a real town school. For nine years I'd been in a three-room school where there were sometimes only three in the class—Leroy Schneider, Alphonse Theis and me. When Kasper consolidated with the Poth district, there were just the three of us from Kasper going into tenth grade. But in Poth, there were 13 in our graduating class. It was a really big class.

It was not hard to make friends. All the girls were very friendly and accepted me right away, especially Crystal. She and I became close friends and stayed that way for years. We wrote each other long letters during the summer. I was out at our farm, usually working in the fields, she in town helping in the family business.

Sometimes we would see each other at a dance, but most of the time we wrote about our dreams, our hopes and our disappointments. She was a deep person. I learned a lot from her. I don't think Crystal ever cheated or lied about anything in her life.

One incident stands out in my mind. During our senior year, in 1949, we had a civics teacher named Mr.

Harper. We all used to make fun of him. He was new that year, and the poor guy suffered our small rebellious ways. I am ashamed to say we treated him badly.

We were facing finals that week, and, as usual, were a little nervous. At lunchtime we were in the study hall, where the civics class was held and also where Mr. Harper's desk was. Some of the boys learned Mr. Harper

had left his final test on his desk and gone to lunch. One boy saw the test, read the questions and told us. I was an A and B student (Crystal got straight A's) and didn't really have to worry, but I decided to sneak a look too, though we were really nervous about it. I had never done anything like that.

Every senior in the room looked at the test, except Crystal. She refused; it was wrong and she would not participate.

Crystal Warnken.

When we took the exam that afternoon, all the class of course passed the test, making from the 70s to the 90s. I think I got an 85. For some reason I couldn't remember all the answers. Well, Crystal was the only one to make 100. That was a lesson I have never forgotten. It made such an impact on me that I told the story to my children and my grandchildren. Cheating does not pay.

I loved to spend the night at Crystal's. It was like being in another world. Her house was beautiful, big, spacious and cool. Her whole family was so nice to me. I loved to laugh and tease with her sisters. I had a secret crush on her older brother, Charles. Crystal and I would stay up late and talk about life, about boys, what we wanted to be when we grew up and about people, but, as always, Crystal said something good about everyone.

Crystal loved music. She played the piano just for the love of playing. Our senior yearbook had a Last Will and

Testament page. It said, "I Crystal Warnken leave my love of music to anyone who doesn't like it." She wanted everyone to love and appreciate music like she did.

I never was very popular with the boys in school. Neither was Crystal. There were so many nights we would sit on the edge of the dance floor and wait for someone to ask us to dance. We'd sit on the benches and talk and laugh and act like we were having so much fun, and all the time this fear was rising up inside that another dance would go by and we would wind up being just wallflowers.

We had another good friend, Jennie Lee, so outgoing and popular. She danced every dance. Crystal and I were so envious. We wanted to be like her.

One night we waited and waited to be asked to dance. Finally one of the boys sauntered over and asked Crystal to dance. I was left sitting there. I felt doubly bad, because the boy who asked her to dance was the boy I liked.

As Crystal looked over her shoulder at me and smiled wanly, I knew what she was thinking. The boy she liked never did ask her to dance that night, so she knew how I felt. I was happy for her. At least she got to dance.

After school, Crystal and I went our separate ways. I went to work in San Antonio and two years later got married. She went to Incarnate Word College in San Antonio, went to nursing school and became a wonderful, compassionate nurse. I wasn't surprised. She was working at M. D. Anderson Hospital in Houston when my sister Gerry had thyroid cancer surgery.

Years later, Crystal moved back to San Antonio and continued in nursing. She married a physician in Austin, the man of her dreams. She and her husband were retiring and building a home near Pleasanton, close to her brother, when she developed a brain tumor. She died shortly thereafter, before they moved in.

Crystal left a wonderful legacy just by living her life. I will never forget her.

19. Sam, the Last One

Sammy—Sam, as we now call him—was my youngest brother, born when I was a junior in high school. It was after the Christmas holidays in 1947, when I was 15, that Mother told us she was going to have a baby.

I must confess I was shocked. After all, there were already seven of us kids. The youngest, Donny, was six. One more in the family? What would people think? Where was the baby going to sleep? Our house was already so small that I slept in a bedroom carved from part of the attic along with my sister Elizabeth, "Sis." There were times when our youngest sister, Gerry, would sleep with us. There wasn't much room in the house for another.

It was quite a while before I told my friends. I was too embarrassed. Finally I told Crystal, who I knew would understand. She was thrilled for my family and me.

I began to look at this new baby in a different light. As summer went by, my mother began to plan. She told my Daddy that this baby was going to be born in the hospital in Floresville, and not at home like the rest of us.

September 11 came. When she went into labor, Daddy took her to the hospital, and that day Samuel Earl Zook was born. Those three days in the hospital were probably the only times in her life my mother got any rest. She loved it. When they came home we were all thrilled to have a new baby brother to spoil.

Sammy was spoiled and precocious, and he talked early. I don't know if it was because so many people doted on him or because God just made him that way.

He had a vivid imagination and loved sports. By the time he was five or six he knew every baseball player,

Sammy Zook with the chickens in 1953.

what team they were on, batting averages, RBI's, home runs, who was going to win the pennant and who was in the World Series.

I remember the summer my Grandpa came to stay with us. Grandpa loved baseball and listened to all the games. He and Sammy both loved the Dodgers. They would sit for hours, their heads leaning toward the radio, and when Sammy's team would win or hit a home run he jumped up and down and yelled at the top of his lungs, while Grandpa would take another dip of snuff and swig of the warm beer from the bottle under his cot, where he would save it all day.

Sammy could sing from the age of two. Not only could he sing, he could also hear a song and sing it from memory with perfect pitch. He had a beautiful voice. He also enjoyed playing the guitar. His favorite guitar was a big stick or an old tennis racket on which he would "play" as he sang "Good Night Irene" or "Rudolph the Red-Nosed Reindeer." This was in 1953, when he was four or five years old. We said then that Sammy was going to be a singer.

He loved baseball and also football. When his brothers were playing football at Poth High School, he didn't miss a game. He was probably their biggest fan, besides my daddy. His dream was to play football too.

But when Mother and Daddy moved to San Antonio and Sammy had to go to school there, he didn't get to play for Poth, which was his dream. He played Little League Baseball, with Daddy helping coach the team, and he was good. But he wanted to play football.

He was about 14 or 15 when he was at Harlandale High School, and he wanted to make the football team so badly. But he also loved drama and singing, so was in the drama department and choir. He had an important role in their musical, "The Music Man." He was really good in that, and his musical ability really began to show. But he still wanted to play football. It was more important!

One morning he left for school and never showed up. The school called that afternoon, saying he was absent and wanting to know what was wrong. No one had seen him since he left the house that morning. There had been no harsh words, nothing said; everything seemed fine. But he didn't come home that night, or the next one, or the next one.

For three weeks we had no idea where he was, or if he was alive or dead. Mother and Daddy were shocked and grieved. Sammy was the only child at home now. Mother enjoyed this child more than any other, for she had a chance to enjoy his life and every childhood growth and change. She never had a chance to enjoy the rest of us, since the seven of us were all so close together.

Mother left a light on in the window and never turned it off. Every night she would sit in a chair by the window and fall asleep waiting for Sammy to come home. I was married by then and had small children, and my heart ached for her. His picture was out on all the TV stations and in the news for several days. It was a horrible time.

Three weeks later, Sammy was found. He had hitch-hiked out to California. He had become overwhelmed with football and the thought that he might not make the team. Things weren't working out at practice. For some reason he couldn't talk to either Mother or Daddy or any-one about it and decided to just run away from home. He couldn't even explain it.

When he got there he found a job at an animal hospi-tal and was given a room in back, but then Sammy wanted to go to school. He went to the high school in Pasadena and tried to enroll, giving them his real name and the name of his school in Texas to get his transcript. Harlandale of-ficials called my parents, and that was it.

The authorities in California asked if he wanted to call his parents, and he said yes. After much crying among them, Mother asked if he wanted to come home, and again the answer was a quick yes. They sent him home on a bus and he went back to Harlandale but never played foot-ball.

Sam graduated high in his class and went on to get a bachelor's degree and also a master's. He went to Viet-nam with the Air Force, and when he came back he lived with my husband and me for a time while he was sta-tioned at Carswell AFB. That gave me the time I missed when he was growing up, because I left home when he was not even a year old.

Sam is now a devoted and loving father and grandfa-ther and still loves football, baseball and basketball. But he is content just to watch it on TV these days. I am not sure he knows all the batting averages and all that. He is still an excellent singer, and has sung at weddings, funer-als, family reunions and solo in church choirs, sometimes with no accompaniment and always on key. But even though he practiced on a stick with two strings, he never learned to master the guitar.

20. Friday Night in South Texas

Autumn in South Texas is not like autumn in New York, or in Michigan or even in Oklahoma. In September we may get a cool front before the month is gone, but sometimes we swelter in the heat until October.

By then the landscape is brown with blowing sand and dust and most things growing have turned brittle—except for the late peanut crops, which stay green. We look expectantly to the north, watching for the dark blue front to blow in and bring cool weather and a shower.

By the late 1940s, my sister Margaret and brother Junior and I were riding the school bus to Poth High School. The one thing we looked forward to was the Friday night football games. As in most Texas towns, it is one of the most exciting social events of the year.

Our school was so small that we had only a six-man football team. The result is probably the fastest, most exciting game in the world since there are so few men on the field. With more offense than defense, the scores are usually pretty big.

Poth's football field was right behind the high school. Everyone walked, or ran, up and down the sidelines to watch the game. There were no stands. The schools didn't have bands, but we usually had a pep squad with drums, even pep squad leaders.

I was a snare drummer. So was my sister Margaret. Gold and blue were our colors. I still remember the feel of the gold silk long-sleeved blouses we had one year with our navy blue skirts. Of course, the skirts were long, to our knees. We wore loafers and navy or gold socks. I felt so good in that uniform.

We practiced marching and cheering all week after school and sometimes before school. Then came Friday afternoon. We didn't have to ride the bus home that day, because we had to stay in town for the game. If we had gone home, we might not get back for starting time since Daddy was always late coming in from the fields.

I would stay with Jennie Lee, Gay, Anna Marie or Crystal—the only girls in my class who lived in town—and walk home with them, and just lie on the bed and gossip and giggle and laugh.

Later we would walk over to Schneider's Cafe for french fries and a Coke, then walk around town to see who else was hanging out. Some of the football players did the same thing, then went back to the locker rooms to suit up.

Finally, we dressed and walked to the school. Margaret often went home with Margie Stavinoha, and they would come back about the same time.

The boys were on the field going through pregame warm-ups. I could feel the excitement. We could see the pickups and cars parking right next to the field, where the farmers and their wives could sit on the backs of the pickups and watch the game. I could smell the hot dogs cooking at the concession stand. Kids were running and squealing and playing tag. The air was usually hot and sultry with a soft Gulf breeze stirring a few mesquites nearby.

It was Friday night in South Texas.

Finally, the coin toss came, and the game started. The game went back and forth, from one end of the field to the other, because six-man football is so fast. I could see most of the men running up and down along the field, trying to keep up with the plays. By the end of the night, my throat was sore from all the screaming and yelling.

Looking down the sidelines, I could see Mother and Daddy with my younger brothers and sisters, who usu-

Margaret, Lois and Elizabeth Zook at the old farmhouse.

ally got there after the first quarter. Some Fridays they didn't get to come—until my brothers Junior (Lawrence), Bob and Donny began to play. Daddy loved football and even played when he went to Floresville High School. My brothers, including my younger brother, Sammy, all played high school football, and Daddy was in his glory. He tried to make every game the boys played in. He was proud of them.

At halftime the pep squad marched on the field. To this day I can remember how to play, although I never played the drum again nor went to many games after my brothers quit playing football in Poth in the early 50's. But I still remember "Pirates Forever! Hail Gold and Blue! You know forever and always, we'll be true to you. So fight, fight, fight, fight boys! Show honor due! To the Pirates Forever, hail to thee, the Gold and Blue!" How come you never forget things like that?

I sang that for my grandchildren. They laughed because they couldn't believe I still knew it.

Going to the away games was even more fun. The best part was afterward we could ride back to Poth on the same bus with the football players. The boys could sit with the girls, and if you had a boyfriend you could sit with him. Most of them did. Crystal and I would almost always sit together and talk. Sometimes I would sit with Jennie, Dorothy Ann or Anna. If we won, we were all laughing and cheering. If we lost, it was quiet.

Sometimes one of the teachers or coaches would take us home, often on the school bus when they took the players home. One night I remember the dust and sand flying in the moonlight, a cool breeze blowing in the bus window and storm clouds to the north. When Margaret and I got out of the bus, I felt it. A norther was blowing in. I could smell rain in the air.

As I looked up and saw the dark clouds scudding across the moon, it was like a promise of change. Tomorrow would be cooler. Monday I would go back to school and the pep squad would learn a new song. Next Friday night the Poth Pirates would win.

I looked at our house and saw a light in one window. Everyone was asleep but Mother, who was probably up reading. I could hear the cows lowing in the pen by the barn and a coyote howling in the dark.

Margaret and I shivered and ran into the house. Winter was coming soon. Next it would be spring, then summer, then autumn again in South Texas.

21. Saturday Night in South Texas

The sun is going down in the west. It is so hot. But it is Saturday night and the dance halls are calling. Every Saturday night there is a dance somewhere in South Texas.

The year is 1948. Last week the dance was at Three Oaks Hall. The week before there was one at Hobson. I never got to go to Hobson—too far away for my brother and me to drive in the old gray 1941 Ford pickup.

But if there was a dance at Three Oaks or at Hermann Sons Hall in Poth, I was gonna go no matter what. I loved going to Hermann Sons Hall. Three Oaks was okay, but I was more familiar with the dances in Poth.

When I was small, I remember going to dances at the Kasper school. The band would consist of a guitar player, a fiddle player or two and maybe a harmonica player. They cleared out the desks and put everything in one room, opened up the big folding doors between the two big classrooms and put up a portable stage. Everybody danced and danced, with cornmeal thrown on the floor to make it slick and easy to slide on.

As small children, we played outside and watched through the windows and from the doors as the grown-ups danced. Before electricity came in the early '40s, when rural electrification came through, they put up kerosene lanterns to light the place up. I loved the sound of the music and the beat of the men's boots and big heavy shoes on the wooden floors.

There have been dances over at Three Oaks since before I was born. My mother and father had their first date going to that New Year's Eve dance at Three Oaks, in 1931. When I left home in 1950, I moved to San Antonio and spent quite a few Saturday nights at Fest Hall, and later on at the Farmer's Daughter.

Just before I got married and even afterward, when my husband and I would go dancing with my aunts and uncle and friends, we went to Helotes to John T. Floore's big dance hall. The outside patio with its spacious concrete floor was wonderful on warm spring, summer and autumn nights. We went to see Charlie Walker, a local singer, and even got to hear a newcomer everyone was talking about. His name was Willie Nelson. A few times I had dates to the Silver Dollar Saloon in Bandera, where we danced the night away, then drove back at 2 a.m. to my apartment in San Antonio.

After moving to North Texas, near Fort Worth, in 1968, we even went to a few dance halls with our grown kids, who loved the old-time country-western dances. Our favorite was Nine Acres Club out in Colleyville. I think I only went to Billy Bob's in Fort Worth one time. By then my dancing days were gone, but I still yearned for the good old times.

But this was 1948. I was 16. And I was going to the dance at Hermann Sons Hall in Poth. I hurried and helped milk the cows. The sweat was rolling down my face and my back. I had to take a bath. Well, taking a bath at our house meant filling up the big wash tub set up in the bedroom and scrunching down in it to bathe. Finally I felt clean, and the breeze through the window cooled me off.

I put on my white cotton peasant blouse and my big full pink printed skirt that swirled when I spun on the floor. I had rolled my hair in pin curlers earlier in the day, and now it was soft and curly. I just hoped the humidity and heat wouldn't make the curls droop too soon. We didn't have hair spray back in those days, so you just had to depend on permanents to keep the curl. And I hadn't had a permanent in a year. It was too expensive. But tonight my hair looked great.

I applied my bright red lipstick and slipped on my sandals, and Junior and I took off in a cloud of dust for Poth. I knew I'd see Crystal, Jennie Lee, Dorothy Ann and other friends. But I was wondering which boys would be there to dance with.

We drove up to the big dirt parking lot, already full with cars and pickups. As we walked in the door of the big white frame building sprawled out under the trees, I could hear the oom-pah of the polka the band was playing. The strong smell of beer was coming from the bar area as I walked into the big hall. The dancers were swirling and dancing round and round the room, and I could see the walls lined with benches, people sitting there, watching the dancers.

Junior took off to find his friends. I began to walk around looking for Crystal or Jennie Lee. Well, there was Jennie Lee dancing and laughing with Paul, her boyfriend, and, oh my gosh, there was Crystal, dancing with some boy. He was happily stepping on her feet, and she was trying to get out of the way and acting like she was having a lot of fun. But I knew better.

I sat down on the bench and waited for the set to finish. She saw me and walked over, smiling and thanking the tall, gangly boy. When she sat down she smiled sweetly and said, "I just couldn't hurt his feelings." I shook my head and smiled, knowing what she meant. We always seemed to be dancing with the wrong boys. The ones we wanted to dance with had girlfriends.

We waited for the "Paul Jones." That is where the girls get in the center and the boys in the outside in a large circle and the music starts. We all walked around in the huge circle, in opposite directions, boys and girls; then the whistle blew loudly and the boy next to you grabbed you and you started dancing. You never knew who you would get, but sometimes I was lucky: the boy was tall and handsome and a great dancer.

I hated when it was over, but we sat back down and waited for the music to start up with Cotton-Eyed Joe. Now that was something we could dance to without a partner. So much fun. We swayed and back-stepped and front-stepped for sometimes two sets, if the musicians were agreeable to doing it again. That was my favorite time.

The night wore on, and the heat in the hall was getting unbearable. Only big fans stirred the air. Not much coolness in the place. The men and the boys who kept going to get beer outside got rowdier, and every once in a while I could hear yelling and hollering as someone broke up a fight. But I seldom went out. I stayed inside, even during intermission. The only ones who went outside were the couples who went to their cars to "talk."

Toward the end of the night, as I was sitting laughing and talking with Dorothy Ann, I could see one boy coming toward me, smiling. My heart jumped. Was he coming to ask me to dance? He didn't say a word; he just reached out his hand and I lifted mine and got up.

The boy I had been hoping to dance with all night was right there before me! We two-stepped around the dance floor, and when he put his cheek next to mine I wanted to faint. Why couldn't this go on all night? Too soon the dance was over. He escorted me to the bench, smiled and walked off.

It was the best dance of my life. The clouds were beginning to build up some in the west. I could see the darkness on the horizon and a streak of lightning. A breeze was kicking up the dust in the parking lot. It was cooler as I stepped into the pickup. Junior started it up and we drove out to the farm.

We talked. I had seen him dancing one time, but he mostly hung around with his friends. After all, he was only 14 years old. He liked the girls but didn't have the nerve yet to dance with them.

"Did you have fun?" he asked. "Did you dance with anyone?"

"Oh, yes,' I said. "I had lots of fun. And I danced a lot!"

He glanced over at me as he shifted gears and started past Schneider's Cafe on the road to home. He smiled. "Oh yeah? Who did you dance with?"

"None of your business!" I said, smiling and tossing my hair. My curls drooped down on my neck, most of them gone. But I didn't care. It was all worth it. I had danced with my secret crush.

22. Leaving Home at Seventeen

I was only 17 when I left home that summer, excited about my new venture in the big city. I left with two suitcases full of clothes and belongings.

Even though I felt a lump in my throat when I looked out the car window as we drove down the dusty lane, I felt a flutter in my stomach. Mother, Daddy and my seven brothers and sisters were waving from the front porch, while two of the dogs ran barking after the car.

I knew I would miss them all, but I had my life ahead of me. I'd come back to visit. Richard Wauson, the principal and teacher for the Kasper School, lived in San Antonio in the summers while finishing his college courses, working long hours at Colonial Bakery at night and going to Trinity University in the day. I would be company for his wife, Lessie, and her little boy, Dickie. They were renting me a room in San Antonio while I looked for a job and signed up for business school.

That was a fun summer. Lessie was like my best friend. We could laugh and giggle and talk about boys. We spent lots of time over at Richard's parents' house in Collins Gardens. Their family was big and lots of fun. Johnny Wauson was my old boyfriend, but I had a crush on Eddie. He was older, dark and handsome, and I thought he looked like a movie star. And he was usually there, so I could daydream about going out with him.

The first week I found a job around the corner from the house they rented on Hoefgen Street. The company was Rowles Sales Co., the Norge Distributor for that area of South Texas. I was thrilled to find that job. I made 35 cents an hour, a lot of money then. After a year, I got a raise to 50 cents an hour. Out of those paychecks I would pay my $10 a week for room and board and the rest for bus fare, Cokes and an occasional movie and dance. Sometimes I even managed to buy a new blouse or shoes.

I didn't make enough to go to business school like I planned. But I progressed in my job, going from office clerk to the bookkeeping department, to being the owner's secretary within two years. Taking shorthand from Nellene Jackson at Kasper School came in handy.

I made friends with a girl named Elsie Hunter. A boy named Jerry who worked there had a little 1947 convertible. We three got to be good friends and hung out together.

Jerry let us drive his car. I could drive, but Elsie couldn't.

Lois Zook at 17.

One day she was trying to drive and drove up into a woman's yard. The woman, who was working outside, screamed and ran in the house. Jerry took over, backed out and we took off. We never went down that street again.

I decided to buy my parents a new electric refrigerator. They'd never had one but used their old icebox. Through Rowles Sales I was able to buy a Norge refrigerator for a discount, and paid ten dollars a month on it. To see that shining white monster in Mother's kitchen when I would go visit made me so happy for her. She was finally living with a modern convenience.

From June 1949 until December 1950 I was a career girl on my own. That fall when Richard and Lessie moved back to Kasper School, I found an apartment in a two-story, colonial-looking home. My room was up on the second floor. Not long ago, I drove down Hackberry Street; it is still there. My office at Rowles Sales Co. was within walking distance. The building is still there, but the little house on Hoefgen is gone. The freeway runs right in front of it now.

I walked everywhere then—to work, the park, grocery store, beauty shop. When I couldn't walk, I took the bus downtown to the movies or Brackenridge Park or to the bus station to catch a Greyhound to Floresville or Poth, where I'd wait for my parents to pick me up for the weekend. The only car ride I took was an occasional date. Even when I started dating my future husband we went everywhere on the bus. He didn't own a car.

Life in the big city was fun just like I thought it would be. I had gotten a taste of city life working in Poth as a waitress at Schneider's Cafe one summer, but when I got to San Antonio it was like going to New York City—big and bright and full of life, and a chance to be what you wanted to be.

23. The Days of Radio

It was a sultry weekend in August 1949. The temperature hovered near 90 degrees already. A small fan moved the hot air around as flies gathered around the back door, where they kept the bucket for the hogs. All kinds of garbage was thrown in to feed to the hogs at the end of the day. In the heat it would begin to smell a little rank.

I had come home for the weekend from San Antonio, where I'd been working since graduation from Poth High School in May. I loved living in the city, but I enjoyed coming home for the weekend sometimes.

Last night, Daddy had driven in to Poth and picked me up at Schneider's Cafe, where the Greyhound bus dropped me off. Mother and Daddy had gone into town to get groceries, and I was home with my brothers and sisters. The younger ones were out playing somewhere as Margaret and I settled down to listen to the radio.

By then we were 16 and 17 and had sort of outgrown the Lone Ranger and Roy Rogers. That morning around 10 we found "Modern Romances" on KABC. After that it was "What's My Name?" At 11 we switched to KTSA for "Theatre of the Day"; we loved drama. Then we listened to "Grand Central Station," which had more intrigue. At first we argued over whether to listen to "Smoky Mountain Hayride" on the other station, but I think I won, since Margaret liked that program best.

Then it was time for lunch. There were too many little brothers and sisters around to hear anything, so we had to wait a couple of hours to listen to "Hi-Ho Jamboree." That stayed on an hour. Then we kept turning the dial to find something else. In the fall the college football games

In 1950 Daddy built this new house, but it still needed indoor plumbing.

would be on, and we would listen to Texas play—they were our team. Sometimes we would get the Brooklyn Dodgers game, but baseball was boring on the radio.

By then the temperature was more than 100 degrees. It was cooler on the front porch in the shade, as a dusty wind would be coming from the south and the dogs would be lying there with their tongues hanging out, panting. I thought about the dance that night over at Three Oaks and wondered who'd be there. Mother and Daddy would be home soon and we'd start cooking supper, as the other kids did the evening chores.

I would have loved some iced tea; but we were out of ice. All we had was a bucket of lukewarm well water in the kitchen, and I hadn't bought Mother a refrigerator yet. Daddy had driven over to a neighboring farm to get a barrel of water to drink and cook with, as usual.

They'd torn down the old house and built this nice three-bedroom one, but they still didn't have indoor plumbing and the water from the well out back was horrible. No one could drink it. They would have to drill another well to get good water, but they didn't have the money for that.

I thought again about the dance. Maybe I'd just stay home and listen to the Louisiana Hayride and the Grand

Ole Opry. I liked Ernest Tubbs; he was supposed to be on. I wasn't interested in the dances at Hermann Son's Hall and Three Oaks anymore. That part of my life was over. Somehow I couldn't really relate any more. And "My Hit Parade" was coming on soon.

I listened to the radio every night. I really liked "Lavender Blue" with Sammy Kaye, "Some Enchanted Evening" with Perry Como, "I've Got My Love to Keep Me Warm" with Les Brown and "Galway Bay" by Bing Crosby. I sure didn't care for "Mule Train" and Frankie Laine. My favorite for the last year, "Now Is the Hour," also our class song, wasn't too popular anymore.

It was almost five. The heat was unbearable. The sun was lower in the sky, but it was still several hours before the air would cool. I could hear the radio as Margaret dialed the stations. The garden was wilted in the sun, the corn stalks were hard and brittle. Buzzards circled down in the field. I wished they'd get here with the ice. A cold glass of tea would taste good. I went inside to see if Margaret found anything on the radio.

Then I saw the cloud of dust coming down the road, the dogs barking. The truck came to a stop under the one mesquite tree that gave a little shade. The younger kids ran out to help unload everything.

I sat thinking about my life in San Antonio—my room in the Wausons' little house, my job, new friends, riding the bus to the movies and going to the Hitching Post with my aunts on Saturday nights I thought about Eddie Wauson, Richard's brother. He didn't know how I felt about him, and neither did anyone else. It was my secret.

I knew I'd stay home that night, visit and listen to the radio with my family. Tomorrow I'd take the bus back to San Antonio, to my new life, my new home. But my family and the farm would remain in my mind and my heart.

24. A Tough Year

In 1956 it didn't rain. The grass all died, the crops failed and even the cows had to be fed prickly pear. Daddy used a pear burner to burn off thorns from the cactus so the cattle could eat the cactus pads.

My mother got a job at the State Hospital in San Antonio. She was 45. It was the first job she had outside the farm. She was an aide and loved her work.

But it was hard on her and hard on the kids still at home. She had to work the midnight-to-seven shift. She left the farm around 8 at night and drove to Floresville, where she carpooled with two other women. She worked all night, then drove back to Floresville and out to the farm. She got in about 8:30 or 9 in the morning, then had to try to get some sleep and take care of things at home.

It was a hard year for Gerry, who was left in charge. She had the responsibility of her little brother, cooking supper and doing all the house cleaning and laundry without running water. She was a senior and missed a lot of football and basketball games and couldn't participate in a lot of school or social functions.

It was especially hard on Sammy, who was eight. He felt lonely, lost and abandoned. That was a tough year for him anyway, because he was in second grade at Poth Elementary. He had Mrs. Matthews, a hard teacher, and didn't think he could make it through. He still remembers it as the worst of his young years on the farm. Daddy was gone all the time, working in the fields. Donny was playing football in Poth and gone a lot, too.

So Mother decided she would stay with Margaret, my sister who was married to Johnny Wauson and living in

Sam follows Daddy on the tractor in 1957, the year he gave up farming.

Highland Hills in San Antonio. She worked six days a week and came back to the farm on her one day off. It was so much better for her, as Margaret lived close to the State Hospital and she could sleep days at Margaret's. Sammy looked forward to the one day a week she came home from San Antonio, but when she left to go back he cried and cried.

The next summer Mother got on the three-to-eleven shift. She moved back home, drove into work in the afternoons and came home late at night. But she was there during the day, which was especially good on weekends. Sammy could see his mother.

By then the drought had gotten so bad that Daddy made the decision to leave the farm. It was the hardest decision he ever made. Loving farming as he did, he felt like such a failure. After 33 years of farming, he gave up. They sold the farm and moved to San Antonio.

Sammy had mixed emotions. He was in third grade. He had Mrs. Sunday for a teacher that fall, he loved her to death and had made new friends. But it didn't take him long to make friends in his new school in South San Antonio. He could play Little League and Daddy helped coach. Mother was near her work and Daddy got a good job as a night watchman in a steel plant.

By then Gerry had graduated from high school and only Donny was going to Poth High. He lived with the McDonald family to finish out the year and play football.

My parents moved away in 1957. That left only my brother Bob to continue the Lawrence Zook family name in Wilson County. But Bob knew better than to try farming. He got a job with the highway department.

I heard our old farm was auctioned off this past week. It made me sad to think that another family could not make a go of it on that old place. I hope whoever bought it will do something great with it. It would make me happy.

25. Our First House

Eddie Wauson was so dark and handsome. He had beautiful hazel eyes and a smile that would melt your heart. I was 18 and he was 25 when we married. He wasn't the tall cowboy I'd dreamed about but a city man, not that tall, who couldn't ride a horse and didn't own a car.

We had a small wedding at First Methodist Church in Floresville and took the train to Austin for a New Year's Eve honeymoon, in 1950. When we got back to our tiny apartment in an old house on Madison Street, in San Antonio's King William district, we sat down and counted our money. We had $1.35, a week's bus fare for both of us.

For two weeks I took the bus to my job on the south side and Eddie took the bus downtown. One morning he called and said he wanted to ride the bus out to have lunch with me at a diner a block from my office. I was thrilled.

But as we were eating lunch, he suddenly said that he'd just gotten another job. When he admitted he'd been laid off from his earlier one before our wedding, I was crushed that he hadn't told me. He said he was afraid I'd think he was a failure if he didn't have a job and didn't have any money, and then I would call off the wedding!

I thought about all those morning we'd kissed goodbye at the bus stop and gone to what I thought were our separate jobs, but now he says he was just looking!

I finally forgave him, and things did get much better after that. His new job was in the purchasing department of Campbell Steel Company. He eventually became the assistant purchasing agent. We moved to a big garage apartment on McMullen Street. Six months after we married, I quit my job as a secretary to start having a family.

Our new house had more room, and a lawn for Trent and Julie.

Once Trent was born we needed more room and a yard for him to play in. In 1954 we finally found a place we could afford on the north side of town, on Trudell Drive in Dellview. It was only 1,000 square feet, but after our garage apartment it seemed huge. We paid only $9,600 for the house. We got a G.I. loan with not much down.

Every day we drove out in our "new" 1947 Dodge sedan to see the lot. We watched the walls go up and the roof put on. It was thrilling to pick out wallpaper, colors and tile for the floors. We even put parquet flooring in the living and dining areas. French doors opened onto a little patio. There was a carport. As I stood at my kitchen window looking across the fields in the back, I was so happy with my little boy running around the house. But it wasn't long before homes were built in the field.

We didn't have central air conditioning, and it was so hot that first summer. But those ten years were my favorite. The neighbors were all young with children. Every night we'd gather in someone's front yard and sit out on blankets and quilts under the stars, as the Gulf breeze began to whip up from the south and cool the night air.

Our kids ran up and down the street playing freeze tag or chasing lightning bugs. No cars came by because every family had only one car and we were all at home. For blocks you could see young couples and children sitting out in yards just like ours, talking and laughing until time to round up the kids for bed. The younger ones got tired, lay down beside us and fell asleep under the stars.

We suffered together a few summers later when our neighbor was killed in an accident at work, leaving a young wife and two children. The whole neighborhood gathered to help her through that tragic time A few years later she married the brother of her next-door neighbor, a widower with five children. We all rejoiced with her as she moved to a little town in South Texas.

We became good friends with our next-door neighbors, Gayle and Gene, whose children were the same age as ours. We had three more children while we lived there, and so did they. On summer nights we sometimes played canasta as our children ran outdoors. We played on the winter nights because the kids went to bed early. Gayle and Gene moved to Houston just before we moved to a larger house. Gayle and I are still friends.

We also grew close to the family across the street. They invited us to St. Mark's Methodist Church on Vance Jackson Road. Eddie helped Jim with the Boy Scouts and took Trent on Scout nights, though he was only three years old. We played cards and went on picnics with Beverly and Jim, and their kids and ours became good friends. Beverly lives in Dallas now, and we keep in touch.

I sang in the choir. Eddie taught Sunday School and was the junior department's superintendent. I also taught, joined the women's group and played softball and volleyball on the church teams. We made more friends as the church grew in 15 years from 60 members to nearly 1,500.

No one had television, so the best entertainment was talking with friends, playing cards or dominoes, going on picnics or reading. The only reason to stay indoors during the hot summer months was to listen to baseball broadcasts, before the days of portable radios.

Then we got our first air conditioner, a window unit installed in the wall to blow down the hall to the bedrooms. We quit staying outside as much on summer nights, and played cards inside with friends.

Then we bought our first TV, a small black and white set. Like a lot of housewives, I got addicted to daytime soap operas. Then came the comedies, and we couldn't miss the westerns. We had the Cleavers, Nelsons and Andersons for new friends, and we saw more of them than our old friends. We became observers, not participants. We stayed indoors more and just waved at neighbors as we went out to the car.

We began to lose track of the couple down the street who went through a divorce; they were the first we knew who divorced. I wonder if the TV had anything to do with it. Maybe they quit talking.

I made curtains for the windows, and we painted the rooms one more time and refinished the parquet floors. We had birthday parties and Mother and Daddy's 25th wedding anniversary party in the back yard. We enlarged the patio, laying some more bricks, and planted some trees. Eddie built a brick barbecue pit near the patio and we planted a peach tree that put out six bushels of giant peaches one year. I became a Cub Scout den mother and had den meetings for two years.

When our fourth child, Kristi, was born in 1964, we knew it was time to get a bigger house. We traded the Trudell house for a larger one near North Star Mall.

I think we were seeing a change in American life, a loss of relationships and communications. Watching Jack Benny made us laugh, but so did he on the radio—harder, and we enjoyed it more. Our "friend" Charles Flocke made us laugh even more. We really didn't need a TV.

26. The Week After Kennedy Was Shot

When John F. Kennedy was killed on November 22, 1962, I was a 32-year-old wife and mother of three living in San Antonio. My husband and I were devastated.

My brother Don and his wife, Pat, came over and we sat staring at the TV. We hung on to the newscasters' every word. We talked about the tragedy and what might happen. We watched as Lyndon Johnson took the oath of office on the plane, with Jackie Kennedy, still in her blood-stained suit, standing nearby.

But we also talked about the Brackenridge Eagles and the Robert E. Lee Volunteers bi-district high school football game to be played in a week. We had followed the Volunteers all year and planned on going to the game, but now we wondered if it would be called off or postponed.

Then someone heard on a newscast that the schools had decided to play the game. Lee had Linus Baer, its leading scorer for four years. Brackenridge, which won the 4-A high school championship the previous year, had Warren McVea, the Eagles' leading scorer. We had seen Baer play, and here was our chance to see McVea.

The tickets were going on sale the next morning at eight. As we talked about who would stand in line for the tickets, we decided maybe we needed to go a little earlier, like 6 a.m.; then we moved it to 3 a.m.

As the night progressed and all we could think about was President Kennedy's assassination, we decided to go on up to Alamo Stadium at about 10:30 and be the first ones in line. It would help take our minds of what was happening in Dallas. My sister-in-law Pat, Trent and I would spend the night there. We got blankets, coats, thermoses of hot chocolate and coffee and drove to the stadium. Our husbands went to bed.

As we drove into the parking lot, we were amazed to see at least 150 people ahead of us in line! As the night wore on, more people came. A guard let us all in the gym about midnight, as it was freezing cold. They lined us up in order as we came in, and we were at the top of the seats in the gym. We spent the night with probably a thousand people, talking with our new friends around us. All we could talk about was the assassination of Kennedy.

By the next day more than 20,000 tickets were gone, and the game sold out a week early. They had to put portable bleachers in the end zones for a crowd of 26,000, the largest crowd yet for a high school game at Alamo Stadium. I spent the week watching the news.

When November 29 finally arrived I didn't feel like going, and I think a lot of people felt that way, but as we drove into the stadium parking lot my excitement picked up. We found our seats, stood for the National Anthem and the school songs and waited for the kickoff. I looked across the field and saw the field of purple of the Brackenridge Eagles fans. On our side was a sea of red and gray.

Lee received the kick and scored before the Eagles got possession of the ball. But that was only the beginning.

We never did get to sit down. There never was a lull. After Lee scored the first two touchdowns, Brackenridge got the ball and scored, and from that time on whichever team got the ball scored. The Eagles' coach put "Wondrous" Warren McVea in as quarterback so he could touch the ball on every play. He ran zigging, zagging and streaking across the field, and before we knew it he would be through all the Lee players to score a touchdown. Or he would loft a beautiful pass. He was the most exciting high school football player I've ever seen.

Warren McVea scored 38 points that night, and Linus Baer scored 37. But Robert E. Lee won the game 55-48. It is still known as the most exciting high school football game in Texas history.

As the team huddled in prayer in midfield after the game, the fans stood and bowed their heads. Silence came over the crowd, and then we all headed for the gates and the parking lot.

Somehow that hometown high school game brought all of us in San Antonio together that night.

27. A Baby Gets Very Sick

Derek was a happy baby, always smiling and laughing. But one week in 1963 we were not sure if he would live or die.

Derek was two years old when he got the mumps. After four days he began to feel better and wanted to play outside, but then began to run a fever. It rose higher as the day went on, and by 4 p.m. it was near 103. He was fretful and crying and not like himself. An hour later it was 104. I called our doctor and got the answering service. The girl assured me the doctor would call right back.

Two hours went by and no call. I called again. Finally about 9 p.m. a doctor called back. Our family doctor was out of town and this was someone taking his calls. I told him the situation. He said, "Look in his throat to see if it is red." I couldn't really tell, but he said, "Oh, I'm sure it's just a sore throat. Give him some aspirin. He'll be okay."

As the night went on, fear began to grip my stomach, because he continued to cry and the fever stayed high. My husband went to bed and I put the other two children to bed, but I stayed up. Finally I walked into the bedroom carrying Derek in my arms and said to Eddie, "I want a doctor to see him. I want to take him to the emergency room. I know he is really sick."

Eddie got dressed and I called Pat, my sister-in-law and good friend who lived down the street, to come stay with the other two children.

In the emergency room the nurse put Derek on the examining table and began to check him out and asked who our doctor was. I said, "My doctor is out of town, and I want a doctor to see him here." She asked my doctor's name and said, "Well, don't worry, we will have a doctor to see him."

I stood by Derek who was crying and very hot. He would fall asleep but then would wake up and start screaming. Eddie and I looked at each other, and I could see the fear in his eyes. I'm sure he could see fear in mine. The nurse came back in and said, "The doctor is on the phone. He wants to talk to you."

Derek with Eddie and me.

I ran down the hall to the phone, and a voice said, "Mrs. Wauson, what is your problem?" I recognized the voice as the doctor from the night before. He asked a few questions, then asked to speak to the nurse. When the nurse handed me back the phone he said, "Okay, Mrs. Wauson, the nurse says he has a very red throat, and I am going to get her to give him a shot of penicillin."

I was so frustrated I started to cry, "He is allergic to penicillin! He can't take that!" The doctor said in irritation, "I'll tell her to give him a shot of sulfa, but it will really hurt him." I was still crying. The doctor asked if I wanted him to hospitalize Derek or what, and I replied that I wanted him to tell me what to do. "I think you are just getting upset over nothing," he said. "He only has a sore throat."

Crying, I hung up and went back to tell Eddie what the doctor said and how the sulfa drug injection would hurt him. Eddie said that we should leave. I could hear the anger and worry in his voice

As we drove home after midnight. Derek was in a deep sleep that scared me. But when we got home, he began crying again, then would drop into a deep sleep before waking and crying again.

At 8 a.m. a friend knocked on the door. I told her about our night. She said, "Call my doctor. He works on Saturdays. He'll see you—I know he will." They said for me to bring him right in.

As soon as we got there the doctor began to examine Derek. As the doctor turned to me I could tell by his eyes it was not good news. "Mrs. Wauson," he said, "I am going to put him into the hospital immediately. He is very sick. He either has meningitis or encephalitis." I asked the doctor if my baby was going to die. He looked at me quietly and said, "We don't know."

The next several hours were a blur of shock and fear and anger. Why wouldn't anyone believe me when I said my child was sick? At the hospital, the doctors and nurses sent Eddie, my mother who'd just arrived and me down the hall to wait for them to do a spinal tap to tell if it was encephalitis or meningitis. I can still hear the screams coming from the room as they did that test. They will haunt me for the rest of my life. I held onto Eddie's hand, and my mother put her arm around me.

When they called us in, the doctor told us it was mumps encephalitis, and there was nothing they could do but wait it out. The spinal tap helped the pain, because he was better after that. He mostly slept for several days, and gradually got better. After several days he sent us home. Derek would live.

It took him several weeks to recover. He had to stay quiet. As weeks and months went by, he began to get better. It took me a long time to forgive the doctors for not believing a mother who knew her child was really sick.

The week after Derek got out of the hospital, a young girl three streets over from us died of mumps encephalitis. My heart grieved for her parents, because I knew that except for the grace of God it could have been my son.

28. Sports and Softball Dreams

Using old boards for bases, the ground hard as a rock and weeds and stickers in the outfield, our softball field at Kasper School was pretty typical for country schools in Wilson County.

I loved playing softball. We had a good team, too, and could beat the other little schools. Henrietta Pundt and I were the only girls on the team. She played outfield and I was the catcher, though I couldn't afford a glove. The only kids on the team with gloves were Billy Haese, the pitcher, and Alphonse Theis, who had a first baseman's mitt and therefore played that position. The rest of us used our hands.

We played fast pitch. Billy could pitch a fast ball, too. I injured my thumb on my left hand one time. It swelled up really big and hurt for weeks. For years when something would hit it, the pain would shoot through my hand. I think it finally healed about 30 years later. But I was thrilled to be selected for the team. I could hit and throw almost as good as the boys. So could Henrietta.

I've always loved athletics, sports and being outdoors. From the time I was a little girl foot racing with my brothers and climbing to the top branches of the trees and playing baseball and football with them, to now, when I only watch the women athletes in the Olympics, sports and athletics have been a highlight of my life.

When we transferred to Poth High School, volleyball was the girls' sport. I lived for volleyball. Going through an old scrapbook, I found clippings from the Floresville paper telling about all the tournaments we won in 1947–49.

Those were good years. We could beat anyone. Jennie Lee Weller was my setter and I was the spiker. Oh, my, I could jump in those days. In my senior year the school selected the Most Popular and Best-Looking students, but I got Most Athletic Girl. Paul Winkler got Most Athletic Boy.

After marriage and children, softball and volleyball became my recreation. During the 14 years we attended St. Mark's Methodist Church in San Antonio I played softball. I was playing shortstop at first, and then one night during practice my husband, who was the coach, hit a ground ball that bounced off a small rock on the dirt and hit me in the mouth. The pain was intense, and it took a long time to heal.

I never played shortstop again but moved to left field and shied from infield grounders. Our team made it to the playoffs many times and won the city title a couple of times.

When Eddie came home from work I had dinner ready. Then we would pack up the kids and head for the games. That was our recreation for years. He sat in the stands with the kids or took care of a baby and watched me play. He loved it. The kids liked it too. They met all their friends at the ballpark and spent their time playing. They seldom watched the games.

After having my last baby, in 1964, in three weeks I was out on the diamond practicing. The coach was horrified. He thought I would surely get hurt and pass out or something. The first game he put me on the bench and wouldn't let me play. I was upset and pleaded with him. He finally put me in the outfield. I hit a double that night, scoring a run for the team.

Years later when we moved to Hurst I found a volleyball team to play on. The games were during the mornings, so I played this in between driving our four kids to different schools and picking them up.

When our youngest daughter, Kristi, was nine, I signed her up to play softball. It was a new girls' league, so they were short of coaches. They wanted me to coach her team. That began 10 years of coaching girls' softball.

During the '70s, women coaches were not very common. The father of the best player on our team, Mr. George, was very antagonistic. He figured I didn't know as much as he did because I was a woman. He came to watch us practice, and I could feel his disapproval.

But as the days went by, he began to change. By the end of the season when our expansion team began winning games, he was my assistant and let me run the team. The next year we did even better and made the playoffs. He said I was the only woman coach he would ever let his kid play for.

When Kristi moved up to the Junior Girls League, I moved up to coach them. Again they gave me an expansion team as the league grew by leaps and bounds. We named our team the Red Sox. Mr. George wanted his daughter to be on my team. I was glad because she was the best shortstop in the league. We could select one player only. We had to draw for the rest of them. Kristi played as a catcher, pitcher and third base. I loved coaching. We could practice three days a week before the season, so that is what we did. I managed to practice one night a week with them and play one night a week in a women's league.

Eddie followed the Red Sox. He was our strongest supporter and never missed a game. At least by then he didn't have little kids to take care of. We played two nights a week and practiced two afternoons a week, plus I played on a team one night a week. My days were full.

The third year of the Red Sox expansion team we made it to the playoffs and earned a spot in the state tournament in Lubbock. The three days we spent there was the thrill of a lifetime. Sixteen Texas teams made it this far.

We didn't win the tournament, but wewon enough games to come in fifth. Kristi hit her first grand-slam homerun. On the ride home, as we were all reminiscing about the tournament someone pointed out that our team had the only female head coach. I had finally made it!

The next year, Kristi couldn't play because she was working after school, but I decided to coach the Red Sox two more years. I was also playing in two tennis leagues. I was considering giving up softball and trying something else, like racquetball. I signed up for lessons. That last year our Red Sox made it to the state tournament again, but we were not as strong. We played three games and came home. I was 50 and was going to give up coaching.

But that August my oldest daughter had a massive stroke and almost died. I dropped everything that year— no softball, no tennis, no coaching, no racquetball. I even quit painting and playing bridge with my friends.

Over the next 20 years I watched Kristi play softball. She became an excellent pitcher, and even played up until a few weeks before one of her babies was born! But I was content to watch.

After all, I had gone from being a barefoot schoolgirl on hard ground with straggly grass and stickers to head coach of a girl's team honored to play in a state tournament. I even had my own glove.

29. Automobiles, Buses and Walking

Sometimes I yearn for the good old days when we didn't have a car. When my husband and I were dating in 1950 we went everywhere on the city bus or the Greyhound bus, or we walked. We walked to the grocery store, to the drug store, or from McMullen Street over to Roosevelt Street many blocks away to visit his brother and his wife. We walked two blocks to take the bus downtown and transfer to the Collins Garden bus to visit his folks on the southwest side of San Antonio.

We took the bus to our jobs. When we wanted to visit my parents on the farm, we took the Greyhound bus to Floresville or Poth and my parents picked us up in their old pickup.

We bought our first automobile in early 1952. It was a 1947 black Dodge sedan. I knew how to drive, having driven a tractor or the pickup on the farm, but Eddie hadn't driven much. His parents never owned an automobile and neither had he. He was in the Navy for three years, and when he came back he lived at home and rode the bus everywhere.

So I did most of the driving and I also taught my husband how to drive. I know he must have hated it. When we drove to Floresville, Eddie would take over the driving. He learned to drive pretty well. Then we had to go take our driver's tests. We passed and we could drive legally.

We graduated to a 1950 gray and white Oldsmobile hardtop and then bought our first brand new car, a bright red 1955 Ford Fairlane. Eddie's brother Johnny and my sister Margaret also bought their first brand new car, a 1955 Chevy, a beautiful two-tone salmon and cream colored auto.

It seemed we always had car trouble. Since Eddie worked all the time, it was my job to take care it. I think I spent half of our young married years sitting in repair shops waiting for the mechanic.

I can remember sitting in an auto repair shop all day when our youngest daughter, Kristi, was about two. We walked a few blocks away to get lunch, then walked some more, just looking, then sat in the waiting room reading old car magazines and staring at the outdated calendars on the walls. Kristi was very patient and took a nap on my lap.

In 1969 when we lived in Hurst, Margaret and her four kids were visiting us from Arkansas when we got a phone call that Eddie and Johnny's mother had passed away. We left early that morning for San Antonio to help with funeral plans. As our two cars reached Temple, our car broke down. We spent four hours having it repaired as the two families waited.

In 1994 we were on our way to San Antonio when my mother was dying. She was in the hospital and all my family gathered to be with her. I left on a Friday morning, hoping I could get there in time to talk with her before she died. When we reached Austin, our car lost power and we coasted into a service station. It was a 10-year-old Pontiac, and we'd gone many years with no car trouble.

We called a tow truck to take us to the nearest repair shop. After being towed in we were told that the head mechanic had left for the day. We waited with an old man who was sort of the night watchman. A huge dog was tied to the fence, my mother was dying, our car wouldn't run, the place was closing down and we were in the most dangerous part of town.

Then we remembered a niece and her family in Round Rock. We called her and found she was also going to the hospital. She picked us up in her van and we got to the hospital in plenty of time to visit with my mother.

The hospital room was filled with at least 25 Zook family members sitting around laughing, talking, eating fried chicken and playing Grandma's favorite gospel music. Mother roused up enough to see us and talk and visit for a while. When someone asked if she wanted them to be quiet and lower the music and the TV, she shook her head. She loved having her family around her. She passed away a few hours later.

Our car was ready in five days, so after the funeral someone took us to Austin and we went on back to Hurst. Two weeks later we bought a new car. But I was not too excited about it. I'd rather take the bus or train.

I've decided I really don't like cars.

30. Going Back to Kasper School

Not long ago Margaret and I went back to Kasper Community to see where we had grown up. It made us sad. Everything is gone. I drove past it because I didn't even recognize the property.

The big white, tin-roofed, three-room schoolhouse with the big front porch, where the girls played jacks, and the L-shaped back porch, where all our tin cups hung in a row by the water cooler, were gone. Torn down and its lumber used to build new houses in Poth, I was told.

Gone too was the huge dirt playground where we'd played games like Dare Base and Red Rover, where the girls played Hop Scotch and the boys shot marbles. The big white outhouses in the back of the schoolyard, one for the boys and one for the girls, had also disappeared.

There is nothing on that piece of land to remind us of those wonderful school days except one raised cistern down by where the teacherage used to sit.

We got out and walked over by the fence. The gate was padlocked shut. Scrawny mesquite trees have grown up along with bushes and cactus in large bunches on the site of the school, now nothing but a desolate pasture. It made me want to cry. But if I listened really hard, not saying a word, I could still hear the shouts of the schoolchildren: "Red Rover, Red Rover, let Lois come over!"

But a huge mesquite tree with two horseshoe-shaped trunks was still there. It was one of the few shade trees on the schoolyard. We used it for tree tag and games like Hide and Seek that needed a home base. It was also a place to sit and eat lunch or hang out in the shade with our friends. I told Margaret about the time I came out during class to go to the girls' outhouse. Sitting in between the old trunks was our little sister Elizabeth, crying. She had done something and this was her punishment—to sit out under the huge mesquite tree and think about her error.

I felt so bad for her and asked what was wrong, but, she couldn't tell me because she was sobbing so hard. When I came back she was crying less, but I couldn't think of a thing to make her feel better. I wish now I'd given her a big hug. When I see her again I'm going to give her a big hug to make up for not doing it then.

There by the school was a gate, and a country lane leading down to the new house my parents built the year after Margaret and I left home. There was a mailbox in the place where for more than 25 years Mother and Daddy got their mail and their San Antonio *Light* or Floresville *Chronicle-Journal*, our only reading material until the bookmobile came to Kasper.

I could see the top of our house over the mesquite trees, and pastures where our peanut fields use to be. We didn't want to drive down and see the house. It hadn't looked the same when we went back about 20 years ago, and I knew I could never go back again.

So we drove down familiar roads, now paved. Most of the old homes are gone, torn down, nothing but farmland. The only familiar thing on the road back to Poth was the store at Dewees. Dewees School used to be across the road, but it was gone, too, moved to the edge of Poth.

The little store looked different on the outside, but inside it was pretty much the same. Most familiar was the stale smell of beer; after a hard day's work farmers still come to have a beer and visit with neighbors before going home. A few groceries sat on the shelves, dusty with age—cigarettes behind the counter, cases of beer in the coolers in the back. Fifty years and nothing had changed!

We had a Coke and headed for home, leaving a bit of ourselves behind. We knew we could never go back again.

31. Fifty Years Is a Long Time

Fifty years is a long time for anything, especially a marriage. My sister Margaret and I can truthfully say we made it. It seems like yesterday that we married the Wauson brothers.

We always did everything together when we were little. We could have gotten married the same day, too. As it was, our weddings were three weeks apart.

When we were little people thought we were twins. There were 15 months between Margaret and me, but we were almost the same size. Both of us were towheaded blondes, with bangs cut across the front, bobbed on the sides and back. Mother dressed us alike in little short dresses. She made all our clothes from pretty flowered feed sacks, and white muslin panties from sugar and flour sacks, washed and bleached until all the writing was gone.

I can't remember when Mother quit dressing us alike. Probably it was when I became stubborn and decided I didn't want Margaret to dress like me. I don't remember exactly when, but I do remember saying to her, "Quit copying me!"

Margaret and I started school together. We were both in the same primer class at Kasper School. She was five and I was six. Finally the teacher moved me up a grade, and I remained one grade ahead of her. For years I thought I was moved up because I was so smart, and that's what I told everyone.

I didn't find out until years later that the real reason was that the teacher got tired of me always helping Margaret with her homework and telling her how to do her math.

Margaret has said that she was always jealous that I was the first to do everything. Just last year when a group of relatives were talking, there was a lot of conversation about us when we were growing up. I was telling about the times I would go to San Antonio to spend the summer with my grandparents and aunts and uncles.

"How come you always got to stay with them in the summer and I didn't?" she asked. I had to admit I didn't know. I figured it was because I was the oldest.

Then she laughed. "Well, I remember one time I got to go up there and you didn't. It was when I had to have my tonsils out, and I got to go to the hospital in San Antonio and have an operation, and you didn't! And I got to be treated with all that special attention, like getting ice cream and all that stuff. And you didn't! I was so glad! And Grandma even bought me a new store-bought dress, too. It was so pretty. I still remember what it looked like."

I guess I never knew I had it so good. Being the oldest and all, I always thought I had it hard.

If we had stayed in the same class, Margaret and I would have been doing everything at the same time, but as it was I was the first one to go on the senior trip, get the class ring and go to the Junior-Senior Banquet. I was the first to go out with a boy, be kissed by a boy, get to work in Poth and stay in town during the summer. I was the first to go to a dance at Three Oaks.

I was the first to have a real boyfriend, too. That was in 1948, and he was a city boy. His name was Johnny Wauson. But in January 1951, three weeks after I married his brother, Eddie, Margaret married Johnny. I guess she showed me. I found out she had always been in love with him. He was her first boyfriend, too. Johnny and I had been going together for over a year. I was crazy about his brother Eddie, and she had a crush on Johnny all that time.

After graduation from high school, Margaret and I lived together in a little apartment in San Antonio on

Roseborough Street. It was the fall of 1950. We both had office jobs.

I started going with Eddie in September when his brother, Richard, maneuvered a scheme to get us together at the Peanut Festival street dance in Floresville. Margaret started going out with Johnny one week later. The Korean War was on and Johnny, who was in the Air Force, got stationed in Virginia right after that.

When Eddie and I married December 30, 1950, in the Methodist church in Floresville, *Our wedding photo.*

Margaret was my maid of honor. Eddie and I went on the train from San Antonio to Austin on our honeymoon.

Two weeks later, Johnny came home on leave and he and Margaret decided to get married. She was only 17, so Mother and Daddy had to sign for her. A few days later, on January 24, 1951, they were married in Alamo Methodist Church. I was her matron of honor.

She and Johnny left immediately on a train to Virginia for their honeymoon. They set up house in a tiny apartment there, while Eddie and I set up housekeeping in a tiny apartment on Madison Street in the King William area of San Antonio.

Margaret had been married only a few months when she wrote me from Virginia. She said, "For the first time in my life, I am going to do something before you do. I just found I am going to have a baby!"

I could feel the joy coming through the letter. I guess it was hard living in the shadow of an older sister who is bossy and a know-it-all and gets to do everything first. I was very happy for her but also a little jealous.

Margaret and Johnny's son, Wesley, was born in October 1951, while his daddy was still in Korea. I had my first baby, Trent, a year later. The two boys were always close, being one year apart, and were a lot like brothers growing up.

Johnny was in the Air Force stationed in Alaska, Michigan and Arkansas, so we didn't see much of them except between their moves. We took a trip to Michigan one summer and to Arkansas one Thanksgiving. Margaret had three more kids, and so did I.

When we grew up we became even closer. We can tell each other anything. We don't have any secrets. We have both been through tragedy and sorrow and good times and bad. Her only daughter, Lynn, died of cancer at the age of 44. It was as if I had lost my daughter, too. My oldest daughter, Julie, had a massive stroke at the age of 27. She was in the hospital for a year and slowly recovered, though with residual brain damage. Likewise, Julie was like Margaret's own.

Everyone in the family has depended on Margaret since Mother and Daddy are gone. Her home is like a haven of rest, and everyone gathers there when the Zook family gets together. I may be the oldest, but it is like Margaret is the oldest now. I don't think she is jealous of me any longer.

I like being in her shadow. It's comforting.